"I'd like to talk to you about your husband Joey."

Mary Jo stepped outside, curious. She perched on one side of the wooden railing. Amy, on the opposite rail, sat a few feet away. In the marina behind the house, light waves on the bay rippled softly as a boat cruised by.

"What's this about?" Mary Jo asked.

"It's not every day that I confront a wife," Amy began, "but your husband, Joey, is having an affair with my sixteen-year-old sister."

Mary Jo was taken aback. "Really?" she said.

"Look," Amy said, "I have proof." She held up the T-shirt in her left hand. It bore the logo of Joey's auto body shop.

Mary Jo shrugged. "Joey gives these shirts to a lot of people," she said, standing up. "That doesn't prove anything. Listen, I'm going to go in and call Joey now. Thanks for coming by to see me." She turned and reached for the door handle.

It was not the reaction Amy Fisher had expected. Suddenly fury engulfed the young girl. Withdrawing the automatic pistol hidden deep inside her pants pocket, Amy raised it to eye level, and pointed it at Mary Jo's right temple. Then she pulled the trigger. . . .

LETHAL LOLITA

A TRUE STORY OF SEX, SCANDAL AND DEADLY OBSESSION

MARIA EFTIMIADES

ST. MARTIN'S PAPERBACKS

LETHAL LOLITA

Copyright © 1992 by Maria Eftimiades.

Full front cover photograph by Don Banks. Photo of Amy Fisher by Cliff de Bear/*Newsday*. Photos of Joey and Mary Jo Buttafuoco by K. Wiles Stabile/*Newsday*.

ISBN: 0-312-95062-4

Printed in the United States of America

St. Martin's Paperbacks edition/October 1992

10 9 8 7 6 5 4 3 2 1

ACKNOWLEDGMENTS

My thanks to *People* managing editor Landon Y. Jones and chief of reporters Nancy P. Williamson for their patience and support. Also, I owe a debt of gratitude to my editor Charles Spicer and his assistant, Liz Weinstock, St. Martin's' managing editor John Rounds, my agent Jane Dystel, and *People* writer Joe Treen.

Chapter One

The 1983 maroon Thunderbird pulled up in front of a white, split-level house next to South Oyster Bay in Massapequa, Long Island. The driver killed the engine and paused, his hands clenching the steering wheel. It was just after 11:30 A.M.

"Wait here," Amy Fisher said to him. "I'll be back."

The high school senior gathered what she needed—a white extra large T-shirt and a .25-caliber Titan. She walked up the driveway and slowly climbed the two front steps. The driver sat motionless in the car, wondering what was going to happen.

The sun poked in and out of the clouds. The promise of hot days was near. It was May 19—just six weeks before Amy's graduation on the football field of John F. Kennedy High School. A summer of beach parties. College in the fall. It should have been an auspicious time for pretty

1

Amy Fisher, the daughter of a prosperous family from nearby Merrick, Long Island.

But Amy Fisher stood on that front stoop, alone with a haunted past and wrenching secrets. She was a desperate young girl on a deadly mission. In a short time all the pain of the last year would climax in a fury she could not control. In an instant the teenager would shatter two families and expose her formidable secrets to the world.

Mary Jo Buttafuoco knew nothing about this slight, unsmiling girl wearing loose-fitting pants and an oversize shirt, her auburn hair tucked inside a baseball cap. The slender blond housewife had been painting lawn furniture on the back deck when she heard the bell. Her husband, Joey, was working at his father's repair shop, Complete Auto Body, in nearby Baldwin. Her children, Paul, twelve, and Jessica, nine, were in school.

Mary Jo wiped her hands on a towel, walked through the house, and opened the screen door a crack.

"Hello," she said. "Can I help you?"

"Are you Mrs. Joseph Buttafuoco?"

"Yes."

"I'd like to talk to you about your husband, Joey."

Mary Jo stepped outside, curious. She perched on one side of the wooden railing. Amy, on the opposite rail, sat a few feet away. In the marina behind the house, light waves on the bay rippled softly as a boat cruised by.

"What's this about?" Mary Jo asked.

"It's not every day that I confront a wife," Amy

began, "but your husband, Joey, is having an affair with my sixteen-year-old sister."

Mary Jo was taken aback. She started to speak, then paused to regain her composure. After all, she did not know this young girl, and she wasn't about to get into a confrontation on her front stoop. Her marriage had had its share of ups and downs in the last seventeen years, but her Joey and a teenage girl? It seemed impossible.

"Really?" she said.

"I think the idea of a forty-year-old man sleeping with a sixteen-year-old is disgusting," Amy continued.

Mary Jo smiled. "Well," she said, "he's not forty years old yet."

Now it was Amy's turn to be surprised. Where was the shock, the anger, the sense of betrayal she'd been expecting from Mary Jo Buttafuoco? Amy shifted on the rail and clutched the T-shirt tighter. She didn't know what to say.

Mary Jo seized control of the conversation. "What's your name?" she asked.

"Ann Marie," said Amy, using the name of a friend.

"Where do you live, Ann Marie?"

"Over in Bar Harbor," Amy replied, waving her hand.

"Honey, Bar Harbor is in the opposite direction. What's this about? Where do you really live?"

"I live on Dolphin Court," Amy said, naming a street just blocks from Berkley Lane, where she lived with her parents.

Mary Jo's questions continued. "Who's that

with you in the car?" she asked, motioning to the Thunderbird.

"My boyfriend."

At this point Mary Jo's patience was wearing thin. "What are you trying to pull here?" she asked, her voice beginning to tighten with anger.

"Your husband is having an affair with my little sister," Amy replied earnestly. "Look, I have proof."

She held up the T-shirt in her left hand. On the front and back was a small yellow racing car and the logo COMPLETE AUTO BODY AND FENDER INC.

Mary Jo reached out and took the shirt. She unfolded the tag in the collar, checking the size. She shrugged. "Joey gives these shirts to a lot of people," she said, standing up. "That doesn't prove anything. Listen, I'm going to go in and call Joey now. Thanks for coming by to see me." She turned and reached for the door handle.

It was not the reaction Amy Fisher had expected, and the teenager was bewildered. This woman was dismissing her—ignoring her charge and walking away. True, the story was not quite accurate. Amy Fisher did not have a sister; she was an only child. There was no Ann Marie on Dolphin Court. It was she, Amy, who had been having the affair with Joseph Buttafuoco. It didn't matter. Mary Jo had tossed off the allegation with aplomb.

Fury engulfed the young girl, and she reacted with meteoric speed. Withdrawing the automatic pistol hidden deep inside her pants pocket, Amy raised it to eye level and pointed it at Mary Jo's right temple. She pulled the trigger.

The bullet entered Mary Jo Buttafuoco's head above her right ear, shattering her jaw and severing the carotid artery. It ripped through her eardrum and came to rest at the base of her brain, behind her right ear, just an inch from her spinal column. In her last seconds of consciousness, as she fell to the pavement, blood streaming from her head, Mary Jo thought, *Shit. The little bitch got me.*

Later, when police picked Amy up for questioning, the teenager would contend that the shooting had been an accident—in anger, she'd struck Mary Jo on the side of the head and the gun fired unexpectedly. But Mary Jo would insist that she was never hit. The first and only thing she felt was a bullet exploding into her head.

Amy Fisher was dazed. Motionless, she stood over her longtime rival—a woman who until minutes before had not even known of the teenager's existence. For nine taxing months Amy had plotted and schemed. Now, at last, the moment had arrived: her lover's wife lay dying before her.

Police believe that Amy tried to shoot her victim again but didn't know how to use the gun. It was quite simple—all she had to do was squeeze the trigger. Instead Amy apparently pulled back the ejector mechanism, expelling a live round. She did it a second time and then a third. Each time Amy recocked the carriage a live round dropped, falling on top of Mary Jo's motionless body. Panicky, Amy Fisher broke the ejector off the gun and threw it into the flower garden below. She reached down and grabbed the COMPLETE AUTO BODY T-shirt still clasped in Mary Jo's hands. She ran to the waiting Thunderbird, and the driver sped off.

It was 11:45 A.M. Mary Jo Buttafuoco would remain in a coma for the next fifteen hours. When she awakened, she would not only help police identify her assailant, she would also face the devastating allegations about the man she'd married.

Chapter Two

Diagonally across Adam Road West, Joseph Slattery sunbathed on his front deck overlooking the bay. The last few weeks had been wintry and wet, but today was glorious. His wife, Josephine, puttered in the kitchen.

On this May morning, the familiar sounds of the neighborhood—crying sea gulls swooping along the water and the murmur of boaters as they tinkered on board their crafts—was shattered.

When he heard the gunshot, Joseph Slattery pushed his hands against the elbow rest and rose from his chair, a bit unsteady. His wife stepped out on the porch as he hurried around the corner, cutting across the grass. From the side of his house, about forty yards away, he saw Mary Jo Buttafuoco slumped on the front stoop. "Call 911!" he yelled to his wife, running across the road.

Trembling, Josephine Slattery stepped back

into the house and reached for the kitchen phone. A police officer from the seventh precinct answered on the first ring. Josephine Slattery told him all she knew: Mary Jo Buttafuoco of One Adam Road West in Massapequa had been shot. "Send an ambulance," she begged. "Hurry."

She placed one more call: to Joey at Complete Auto Body.

"Come home—it's an emergency," she said hurriedly.

"What's wrong?" Joey asked.

"Just get home!" Josephine practically shouted.

Joseph Slattery dropped to his knees beside Mary Jo. Blood from the severed carotid artery rushed from her head and stained the elderly man's shirt and shorts. To his horror, Slattery, a retired cop, could see the bullet-size hole in Mary Jo's skull. He pressed a cloth against Mary Jo's temple and uttered a quick prayer. He listened for a heartbeat and checked to see if she was breathing. Holding the compress against the wound with more force, he peered up Adam Road West, searching anxiously for the ambulance.

His wife hurried to his side, trying to remain calm. The Slatterys looked at one another in disbelief. They had lived on Adam Road West for almost two decades. They loved the quiet of Massapequa, especially their Biltmore Shores neighborhood, with the beauty of the bay just outside their door. It didn't seem possible a peaceful weekday morning had been shattered by gunfire, that someone wanted Mary Jo dead.

The couple were friendly with all their neigh-

bors but felt a special attachment to the Buttafuocos. Over the years they'd watched Paul and
little Jessie grow, tearing around the corner on
their bikes at breakneck speed and splashing in
the bay with their friends. On summer weekends
they occasionally joined Joe and Mary Jo aboard
the couple's thirty-one-foot power boat, *Double
Trouble,* for a cruise up Massapequa Grand Canal
into South Oyster Bay.

Within minutes of the sound of a gunshot,
residents began pouring out of their homes and
the Biltmore Shores Beach Club, next door to the
Buttafuoco home. Tom Monahan, another retired
cop, had been waxing his car when he heard the
bang. "What the heck is somebody doing, shooting off a gun?" he asked his wife, Pat.

Two miles away on Merrick Road, the main
artery in Massapequa, merchants stepped outside
their stores and watched as an ambulance and
squadron of police cars sped through red lights,
sirens wailing, and made a sharp turn on Bayview Avenue. Careering past St. Rose of Lima
Catholic Church, the Buttafuocos' parish, the
emergency vehicles headed for Adam Road West.

It would be days before Massapequa residents
would hear the disquieting details of what led to
the shooting of Mary Jo Buttafuoco. The news
would rock the serenity of the upper-middle-class
town of beach clubs, boats, and neighborhood
parties. First in a whisper, then in a thunderbolt
of sordid pronouncements, the story spread from
Long Island's south shore to the front pages of
the New York City tabloids and then around the

world. Mary Jo Buttafuoco's painful odyssey was just beginning.

The ambulance arrived shortly after noon. The emergency team sprinted across the grass to the doorway, and the small group of neighbors encircling Mary Jo stepped back. The team checked Mary Jo's vital signs. Her blood pressure had dropped perilously. She showed signs of neurological impairment and was completely unresponsive. Mary Jo was near death. The emergency team radioed for a police helicopter.

Within minutes a helicopter took off from a landing field near Nassau County Medical Center in East Meadow, about ten miles away. It made the trip quickly, landing on the beach next door to One Adam Road West. Paramedics inserted an intravenous line to stabilize Mary Jo's blood pressure and loaded her into the helicopter.

At that moment a white Lincoln Town Car raced down Adam Road West and screeched to a halt. It was Joey and his older brother, Bobby. They'd made the ten-mile trip from Complete Auto Body in record time.

Bright yellow police ribbons cordoned off the Buttafuoco home. Joey ducked under the ribbons and jogged across the grass.

"What's going on? What happened?" he kept asking.

A crowd of neighbors stepped aside, nervous.

"Joey's here, Joey's here," they murmured.

Joey Buttafuoco stopped when he saw the huge bloodstain on his front stoop. His heart began to race. He turned to the ambulance. It was empty.

Then he gazed down to the beach next door. He saw the helicopter . . . and the stretcher.

Joey began to run. His brother and the police took off after him. As he approached the helicopter he recognized his wife, her feet sticking out beneath a white sheet. Mary Jo's blond hair was disheveled and soaked with blood. Joey knew at once she'd been shot.

Police officers and Joey's brother, Bobby, tackled him, trying to pull him away from the spinning blades of the helicopter. Joey tried to push them off: he needed to be at Mary Jo's side. Bobby held his brother tightly, trying to calm him. The brothers, just two years apart, had always been close. They'd worked side by side at Complete Auto Body since graduating high school.

On the sand that day in Massapequa they watched in disbelief as the helicopter lifted off, carrying Mary Jo Buttafuoco to a waiting fleet of doctors. They waited until it disappeared from sight.

"It's not good," someone was saying. "It's not good."

The trip to the hospital took only a few minutes. A little more than an hour after she was shot, Mary Jo Buttafuoco was surrounded by doctors battling to save her life.

It was a busy morning at Complete Auto Body and Repair in Baldwin. Mechanics tinkered with dented Hondas and touched up paint on Cadillacs. In the side office adjusters penned estimates for waiting customers. Cars filled the garage and spilled onto the street and in the lot behind the shop.

Caspar Buttafuoco, seventy-seven, had built Complete Auto Body into a thriving business in the last forty years. An outspoken, irascible man, Caspar was proud of his family. His oldest son, Bobby, was his partner in the business. Joey, the baby of the family, supervised the mechanics. Father and sons arranged their desks in the same corner of the office, at a right angle, with Caspar in the middle. Lining the window ledge of the shop, dozens of Joey's weight-lifting and arm-wrestling trophies were on display. Photographs of Joey, Mary Jo, and the kids hung from the office walls.

When the telephone rang around noon that day, and the receptionist motioned to Joey, Caspar Buttafuoco had watched his son's reaction in horror.

"I've got to fly out of here," Joey said abruptly, putting down the phone. "My neighbor said there's an emergency."

Caspar Buttafuoco waited anxiously in the shop. He tried to work but couldn't concentrate. What could be wrong? Was it one of his grandchildren? His daughter-in-law? He paced the office of Complete Auto Body, eyeing the telephone.

When the phone finally rang and Caspar heard the terrible news about Mary Jo, the elderly man got right to work, sitting behind his desk and telephoning relatives. He first contacted the Catholic rectory where Pat Connery, Mary Jo's mother, worked. Caspar asked to speak to a priest.

His voice steady, the elderly man explained what he knew and implored the clergyman to break the news to Pat Connery. There wasn't any time to waste.

Within minutes Pat Connery, her husband, Francis, and their twenty-seven-year-old daughter, Eileen, were on their way to Nassau County Medical Center in nearby East Meadow. When the Connerys met the Buttafuocos outside the waiting room of the second-floor intensive care unit, the two families, pale and trembling, embraced tearfully.

They assembled in a special area set aside for families who request privacy. Everyone's eyes were red from crying. So many questions, so much confusion. Grief, fright, and incredulity hung over the small room. A Catholic cleric stood in the corner, ready to offer last rites. He waited quietly, respectfully, on hand if anyone needed his support. On this afternoon, however, the Buttafuocos and Connerys seemed mostly to take comfort in each other.

Before he left for the hospital, Caspar Buttafuoco called Michael Rindenow, a close family friend for the last seventeen years. Michael, an attorney, was like an adopted son to him. Their conversation was fast.

"Mike, Mary Jo's been hit," Caspar said.

"Bad?"

"Very bad."

"Where?"

"Head."

"Where is she?"

"Nassau County Medical Center."

Rindenow's office was less than two miles away. The heavyset man immediately put aside his work and headed to the parking lot. He suddenly realized he didn't have his car. He had just come from a funeral; his wife had dropped him at work. Rindenow hurried into the next office and borrowed the keys to his partner's Mercedes.

Five minutes later, he pulled into the Nassau County Medical Center visitors' parking lot. In the lobby, Rindenow was stopped at the front desk.

"Only family is permitted," the receptionist said.

The attorney tried to explain—he'd known the Buttafuocos since he was a teenager. He was just like family.

The receptionist was firm. Rules were rules.

Disheartened, Michael Rindenow began to walk away. Just then the attorney recognized a hospital security guard, a former client. The guard quietly led Rindenow to the second floor, where he joined the others: Joey, Bobby, Caspar, Pat, Francis, Eileen, and two detectives. It was going to be a tense day.

Doctors gave Mary Jo a blood transfusion and ran an MRI, trying to see where the bullet had lodged and what its destructive path had done. Their evaluation took almost two hours. It was shortly before 3:00 P.M. when a neurosurgeon entered the waiting room. The Buttafuocos and Connerys stood expectantly.

Mary Jo, they were told, needed immediate surgery. The bullet had caused a great deal of harm and might possibly be too dangerous to remove. Surgeons hoped to repair the carotid artery and examine the base of her brain.

It didn't look good.

"If we don't operate, she'll be dead within twelve hours," the doctor told the grieving family. "If we do operate, there's no guarantee that she'll wake up. And if she does wake up, there's no guarantee that she won't be paralyzed."

Permission to operate was needed. The responsibility to sign the paperwork fell to Joey Buttafuoco. The burly six-footer glanced over the form and scribbled his name. He slumped on a chair, emotionally wearied. Questions swirled around him. Who had shot Mary Jo? Why? Why would anyone want Mary Jo dead? Joey kept saying he didn't know. He didn't understand it, not at all. He had no idea who'd done this. His family—his father and Mary Jo's parents—believed him.

Chapter
Three

Amy Fisher was shaking. She and the driver of the maroon Thunderbird tore out of Biltmore Shores onto Merrick Road and headed west. Amy tried to stay calm. The driver was no help; he was petrified himself.

Peter Guagenti, a twenty-one-year-old auto supply worker from Bensonhurst, Brooklyn, was in more trouble than he could comprehend. A gangly young man from a close-knit Italian family, Guagenti had been in a minor jam with police as a teenager, but this was clearly something else. As he drove Amy the seven miles from Massapequa to her parents' home in Merrick, his mind was racing. Had anyone seen him or noticed his car? Was that woman dead? Why had he ever gotten involved in this!

Amy was thinking hard, too. Could Mary Jo Buttafuoco survive a bullet to her head? How would Joey react? She looked down at her jeans and T-shirt, damp with blood. There was a lot to do.

The Thunderbird tore down Hewlitt Avenue and made a sharp left on Berkley Lane. Amy got out of the car and hurried up the walk, still clutching the white COMPLETE AUTO BODY T-shirt. Guagenti sped off to Brooklyn. As Amy fumbled with her keys at the door, her puppy, Muffin, greeted her arrival with excitement, barking wildly. Usually no one was around this early in the day.

About the time Mary Jo was flown to Nassau County Medical Center, Amy Fisher pulled off all her clothing and got rid of it. She changed and hurried to her car, a black 1990 Chrysler LeBaron convertible that had been a gift from her parents the year before.

Police believe that Amy Fisher then attempted to manufacture an alibi. She dropped in on a friend who worked as a hairdresser nearby and chatted for a while. She drove to Nassau Community College, where she hoped to study marketing, and registered for the fall semester. She managed to act normally. No one, not even her parents that evening, noticed any difference in her behavior.

Meanwhile the Buttafuocos and Connerys waited all night in the hospital, restless for news of Mary Jo's condition. It was past 10:00 P.M. when neurosurgeons emerged from more than seven hours of surgery. They were not optimistic. They had managed to control the bleeding by tying off the carotid artery, but Mary Jo had suffered a mild stroke during surgery, and her condition was still critical. The bullet's location made it too risky to remove. If she lived, the bullet would probably remain at the base of her skull for the rest of her life. Doctors told the disheartened family no one could predict what the next twelve hours would bring.

But Mary Jo Buttafuoco surprised everyone. At 3:00 A.M., just a few hours after surgery, she began to moan, fighting off the effects of anesthesia. A nurse stationed in her room hurried to her side. Mary Jo tried to talk but couldn't. Doctors had pushed a tube down her throat and into her trachea, hooking her up to a respirator.

Mary Jo motioned for a pen and a yellow pad hanging on a chart next to her bed. The nurse brought it to her and placed the pen between her fingers.

"Was I shot?" Mary Jo wrote painstakingly.

"Yes," replied the nurse.

"Why?" she wrote.

Mary Jo didn't wait for an answer. She closed her eyes, drifting back to sleep.

An hour later Joey entered his wife's room. He'd been checking on her repeatedly throughout the night. At once he noticed the pad. Mary Jo's words were written exactly on the lines.

Wow, this is a real fightin'-Irish girl, he thought.

With the nurse's help, he gently roused his wife. She looked at him, her eyes questioning.

"Who did this to you?" Joey asked quietly. "Mary Jo, I'm going to hand you a pad and you're going to write it down."

19

He put the pen in her hand. Mary Jo slowly wrote. "A nineteen-year-old girl."

"A girl shot you? Are you sure it wasn't a guy?"

Again Mary Jo wrote, "A nineteen-year-old girl."

"Do you know her name?"

"Ann Marie."

"Where does she live?"

"Dolphin Court."

"Why?"

Mary Jo gazed at her husband, her face contorted by pain.

"I'm suffocating," she wrote, closing her eyes.

Joey Buttafuoco's head was spinning. While Mary Jo was in surgery, his father, brother, and Rindenow had spoken to him in hushed tones, asking if perhaps the shooter was someone from his past, a man bent on revenge. Joey'd had a somewhat checkered background. In the mid-1980s he had dabbled in drugs.

The others reminded him of another incident the previous fall, when shots had been fired into the living room of one Adam Road West, shattering the picture window. The men believed the attacks were related.

Joey thought so, too. But he knew something the others didn't: Mary Jo's assailant was likely someone from his present, not his past. That morning in his wife's hospital room, Joey's worst fears were realized. When his wife wrote "nineteen-year-old girl" Joey swallowed hard. He knew immediately who Ann Marie really was.

Several years ago Joey was an extra on a few

segments of a network daytime soap opera and even auditioned for a role. At this moment his acting talent was in great demand. The repairman braced himself for the performance of his life.

Joey reached for the telephone and called detectives at Nassau County Homicide Division. "You'd better get down here," he said urgently, glancing at his wife. "Mary Jo says it's a girl who shot her, not a guy."

Detectives arrived later that morning but elected to wait until almost 5:00 P.M. to question Mary Jo, wanting doctors first to remove her from the respirator. That evening, in a guttural, almost unrecognizable voice, Mary Jo recounted the scene on her front stoop, verbally sketching a picture of the slight, auburn-haired girl with the T-shirt. Joey, the detectives, and Joey's brother, Bobby, were by her bedside.

What happened next is in dispute. Detectives say that Joey Buttafuoco broke down in tears and admitted he knew who had shot his wife: Amy Fisher, the teenage girl he'd been having an affair with for almost a year. Joey now says that's not true. He insists he never told police he'd had sex with Amy Fisher. He knew the identity of Mary Jo's assailant because he had given away just one white COMPLETE AUTO BODY T-shirt, and that was to Amy Fisher. He says he knew Amy casually from business at the auto body shop—and nothing more.

Detectives tracked down a photograph of Amy. Mary Jo identified her at a glance. Meanwhile

Amy Fisher spent the morning in school. The atmosphere at John F. Kennedy was upbeat and restive. As seniors buzzed about upcoming prom night activities and fretted about regents exams, Amy tried to concentrate. Her fifth-period English class ended uneventfully, except for one benchmark: the buzzer sounded almost exactly twenty-four hours after Amy had fired the .25-caliber automatic.

Amy was too uptight to go home. Many afternoons she headed to Complete Auto Body to visit Joey. Today she didn't dare. She got together with a girlfriend, and around 6:00 P.M. they went to Future Physique, the gym Amy had joined at Joey's suggestion four months earlier. She didn't bring her workout clothes. She only wanted to visit Paul, the twenty-nine-year-old co-owner she often confided in about her relationship with Joey.

As soon as he saw her, Paul knew something was wrong. Amy looked pale and tired. "You look white as a ghost," he said. "What's the matter with you?"

"My stomach," Amy said weakly. "I went to the doctor last week with my mother, and I thought I was better, but I guess I have to go back again. I have my period, too."

They were interrupted by the desk manager, who lived a few doors away from the Buttafuocos. He was waving a copy of the Long Island newspaper *Newsday,* open to a story about the shooting of a Massapequa housewife. Next to the brief article was a picture of Mary Jo Buttafuoco.

"Can you believe this?" he said, to no one in particular.

Paul turned to Amy. "Did you talk to Joe?"

Amy shook her head. "This is no time for me to go there," she said.

"Why didn't you tell me about this before?"

"I just got here."

Paul picked up the newspaper and gave her a playful poke. "I thought you said you didn't care about him anymore."

Amy laughed.

For just a second Paul thought, Could it be? and then he brushed it aside. They went upstairs to Paul's office—a dusty enclave of worn couches overlooking the training room. Edgy and uncomfortable, Amy didn't stay long. Her confidence had begun to falter.

The next day she cut school. She didn't know it, but Mary Jo Buttafuoco had been removed from intensive care. Her prognosis was improving; Amy's freedom was nearing an end.

Late that afternoon Amy's beeper went off. She looked down and caught her breath. The last three numbers were 007. It was Joey. As he had for the last nine months, he had used their secret code.

Amy called him back immediately, only Joey wasn't the only one on the line. Detectives from the Nassau County Homicide Division were listening, too.

Joey and Amy talked for a few minutes. "It's just terrible what happened," Amy said. "Everyone I know is saying the Mafia did it."

Joey suggested they meet, but Amy turned him down. She told him she couldn't make it.

Minutes later, however, Amy went out—exactly what detectives hoped she'd do. Her parents had just returned from work. After changing into a jogging outfit, she told them she was going for a run in nearby Long Beach, along the boardwalk. As the screen door slammed, Amy promised to be home in an hour.

Detectives were waiting down the block from Berkley Lane, a few hundred yards away. Amy slipped behind the wheel of the LeBaron and deftly pulled off the jogging outfit; underneath she wore faded blue shorts and a white T-shirt. She headed north to Merrick Road. She needed to drive for a while and clear her head.

The police car followed her for about a mile and then, lights flashing, pulled her over. It was 6:50 P.M., Thursday, May 21, fifty-two hours after the shooting of Mary Jo Buttafuoco. Her expression defiant, but her heart beating rapidly, Amy Fisher was taken to police headquarters in Mineola for questioning. A day later she was arrested for attempted murder, assault, and criminal possession of a gun. The next time her parents would speak to their child, she was in jail.

Chapter
Four

The shooting of Mary Jo Buttafuoco didn't make the news for four days in New York City, and even then it received only meager attention. But slowly over the next few weeks the secret life of her would-be killer ignited a firestorm of interest. Daily revelations began appearing on the front pages of the city's tabloids.

The motive for the shooting was as mysterious as the auburn-haired assailant. Police immediately labeled the incident a case of "fatal attraction." Infatuated with Joey Buttafuoco, Amy Fisher had jealously tried to kill Mary Jo after Joey attempted to end their affair.

The media latched on to the moniker with glee. For the last two years the New York press corps had followed another "fatal attraction" case—the trial of Carolyn Warmus, a twenty-nine-year-old Westchester schoolteacher charged with pumping nine bullets into her lover's wife. Through two trials—the first ending in a hung jury—the

Warmus story offered the fascinating and irresistible paradox of a young woman from an affluent family going so utterly wrong. With Warmus only days earlier having been convicted for the murder of Betty Jeanne Solomon, the timing couldn't be better. Amy Fisher stood poised to take Carolyn Warmus's place. A new case of a love-crazed killer. That the assailant was this time a teenager only added to its appeal.

For Nassau County detectives, the attempted murder of Mary Jo Buttafuoco couldn't be more straightforward. In announcing Amy's arrest, Homicide Detective Sergeant Daniel Severin spoke at a press conference and condensed the entire story to a sound bite. "She wanted him, and he didn't want her anymore," he said. "If she couldn't have him, no one else could. She was obsessed with him. It was a near fatal attraction."

At the time the explanation, while simplistic, seemed to fit. What else could explain such a vicious, aberrant reaction to Mary Jo's refusal to believe Joey had been unfaithful?

The media were convinced as well. Local television stations and newspapers began running a "Teen Attraction" logo when talking and writing about Amy.

Yet despite exhaustive reporting by the tabloids and local news programs, the central figure in this case remained an enigma. No one could answer the most perplexing question of all. Who was Amy Fisher? A lovestruck ingenue, desperate for attention? Or a hardened temptress, willing to stop at nothing to possess the man she craved?

There was much more to learn about Amy Fisher and how her association with Joseph Buttafuoco was the prologue to a year-long exposure to celestial heights and devastating descents. As fragments of the summer before her senior year in high school unfurled, the stark image was of a teenager's life spiraling out of control, picking up speed toward a deadly finale.

Those who knew Amy Fisher combed their memories of the bright, energetic teen for clues of the obsession that had almost led to murder. They pondered a shocking disclosure that seemed as unthinkable as attempted murder: that shortly after meeting Joe Buttafuoco, the lithe, reserved young woman had embarked on a lucrative after-school job—as a prostitute.

No one understood what had happened to Amy. Sadly, it was the untold tragedy of the morning of May 19: that those who knew and loved Amy most had neglected to pick up the clues she'd so diligently left behind. It was all there. Poor socialization. Low grades. Intense jealousy. Promiscuity. And, finally, a disturbing fascination with violent crime—an admiration for gangs, hitmen, and spys. Somewhere in the last year Amy Fisher had blithely followed Joey Buttafuoco on a detour to unequivocal disaster.

About the same time Joseph Buttafuoco proposed to Mary Josephine Connery in Massapequa, Long

Island, another joyful event took place just a few miles away: the birth of Amy Elizabeth Fisher.

Her parents, Elliot and Roseann, were enchanted. The birth of their daughter, when Rose was just twenty-one and Elliot, thirty-nine, realized their dreams. The couple had only recently married, defying naysayers who believed their eighteen-year age difference would prove too problematic. They also had to contend with disapproval over their different religious backgrounds. Elliot, a Brooklyn native, was raised Jewish; Rose, who grew up on Long Island, was Italian-Catholic.

With the new baby at the center of their lives, Elliot and Rose Fisher looked forward to a promising future. Amy, the only child the couple would ever have, made them a family.

When Amy was four months old, the Fishers moved into a four-bedroom, brick-and-white-shingle high ranch in the Mandalay section of Wantagh on Long Island's south shore. The neighborhood was quiet, tree-lined, an all-white, middle-class enclave near the beach. The three roads in the area—Bayview, Riverside Drive, and Mandalay Beach Road, ended at a marina where the more well-to-do residents docked boats. On summer weekends the local children pedaled down to the corner on bikes, watching the power boats motor in and out of the pier.

One of the draws of the area was its well-regarded school system. In Wantagh Elliot and Rose Fisher hoped Amy would get a solid start on her education. Mandalay Elementary School was convenient as well—just around the corner from Mandalay Beach Road where the Fishers lived. Every morning Elliot or Rose watched carefully as their little girl turned the corner and a crossing guard guided her safely across the street.

In the early grades, Amy liked school. Mandalay Elementary was spacious and bright, with two big playgrounds, a wooden jungle gym, and old tires to swing in. From the grassy mound on the south side of the school, masts of sailboats on the bay could be seen in the distance, and on a windy day salt water caught the breeze.

Pink, purple, and yellow paper butterflies are now stenciled to the kindergarten window where Amy once fingerpainted and sang songs. In the lobby a plaque greets visitors: "Home & School— A Partnership."

It is the kind of place where parents fill the auditorium on open-house night, concerned about their child's reading skills or difficulties with math. They attend school board meetings and vote for candidates who promise to fight for smaller classes and better teachers. They have dreams for their children, not unlike the ones Elliot and Rose Fisher had for Amy.

A year before Amy was born the Fishers opened Stitch 'n Sew, a discount upholstery shop in the working-class section of Freeport, less than two miles from Complete Auto Body. For a few years previously, Elliot Fisher had run a smaller, similar business nearby. When he noticed that the sundries shop on West Main Street in Freeport had closed, he met with the landlord and negotiated a deal to take over the lease. The new space was perfect: a roomy corner store on a busy boulevard, with plenty of parking in the lot next door.

Elliot and Rose worked well together, forming a friendly, diligent team. Elliot managed the store—measuring and cutting fabric and working the cash register. Rose did most of the custom work—sewing drapes and slipcovers and reupholstering furniture. The couple spent long hours at the shop, six days a week. Rose especially was almost always logjammed with orders. Often she went in before the store opened at 10:00 A.M. to get a jump on the day.

Over the years, Stitch 'n Sew grew prosperous. The Fishers painstakingly built a reputation for quality work at fair prices. They began to invest profits in stocks and bonds, setting aside for Amy's education and their retirement. Elliot began to spend more time handling the family finances.

The Fishers arranged for baby-sitters to care for their daughter in the afternoons after school and in the summer, they sent Amy to camp. As she approached her teens, Amy began to fend for herself, checking in by phone with her parents after the school bus brought her home.

Growing up, Amy was chubby and wore glasses. She'd had a serious eye injury as a youngster, leaving her vision in one eye slightly blurred. It is a problem that still plagues her today.

In Wantagh she had a dog, fish, hamsters, even lizards. She played soccer and softball in the field behind the Mandalay school and swam in the town pool. Elliot and Rose signed her up for piano lessons and proudly hung her artwork on the walls. Amy always loved to paint and draw.

She had a few friends but never clicked in any one particular group. Some of her former classmates recall Amy Fisher as a consummate attention grabber who'd take any dare, no matter how absurd. Once, on a challenge from a classmate, she showed up at school wearing a clown's wig.

Coveting attention appeared to be a personality trait Amy never outgrew. Just a few months before she was arrested, she dyed her hair burgundy, then promptly headed over to the auto body shop to show Joey. He shook his head and chuckled.

"Don't you like it?" Amy asked. "It's different."

At school, classmates kidded her good-naturedly. "We made fun of her, you know, teased her about her purple hair," said one senior. "She didn't care. She just laughed."

Throughout her life Amy Fisher had little trouble getting what she wanted. As a child, Rose and Elliot showered their daughter with gifts. "If there was a new toy out, she'd have it the next day and bring it in to show off in class," recalled John Valentino, eighteen, a former elementary school classmate.

It was the equivalent a decade later. Many who knew Amy believe her parents had trouble saying no to her. A few days after she turned seventeen, Amy had an accident with a 1989 white Dodge Daytona her parents had given her the year before. Joey Buttafuoco laughed at the Fishers' idea of punishment for their daughter. "Mr. Fisher was going to teach her a lesson—if she wanted to drive, she had to drive the Cadillac," the repairman recalled.

Six weeks later Elliot Fisher bought his daughter a practically new black 1990 Chrysler Le-Baron, complete with a CD player, cassette deck, cruise control, road wheel tires, and a dark gray interior. The car, just eight months old, had been traded in at ABC Chrysler in Valley Stream two days earlier. It had only two thousand miles on it.

"He liked it—he said it was just what he'd been looking for to give his daughter," recalled Gerard Broschart, the general manager of the shop. The next day Elliot brought Amy to see the car. Broschart gave them the keys and dealer plates, and father and daughter took the LeBaron for a test drive on the parkway. When they returned, Elliot wrote a check for $13,000. Amy picked up the car four days later. "She was very thrilled," said Broschart.

"This girl had everything she could possibly want," added Stephen Sleeman, a twenty-one-year-old who knew Amy well and emerged as an important figure after her arrest. "She had the car. She had a kickin' stereo—it was huge—a color TV, her own phone line, clothes galore. She always used to say 'I can have anything I want. I can do anything I want. It's great.' She liked it that she was an only child. She'd say 'Now I get everything.' "

One thing she didn't get was to stay in her

childhood home. By the time Amy graduated sixth grade at Mandalay and transferred to Wantagh Middle School, Elliot and Rose Fisher had begun to talk about buying a bigger house. They also considered extending the top floor of their present home and filled out applications for the necessary permits.

The Fishers were undecided. Amy was not. She was reluctant to leave Wantagh. The friends she'd made at Mandalay had almost all moved on to the local middle school. Life on Mandalay Beach Road was familiar and safe.

But Elliot and Rose Fisher eventually toured a $360,000 house in nearby Merrick that seemed ideal—a large, two-story split level, with a two-car garage, on a secluded dead end. A rhododendron blossomed in the front yard. The Fishers were charmed by the area. Merrick, a 10.5-square-mile stretch of upper-middle-class houses with tidy lawns and freshly trimmed shrubbery, was decidedly a step up from Wantagh. Just down the block from the new house, on quiet Berkley Lane, was Hempstead Bay. The neighborhood was also a few miles closer to Stitch 'n Sew.

The Fishers went to contract just as Amy completed the seventh grade. Elliot and Rose did their best to reassure their daughter about the move. They drove her to see the new house and toured around the area. Her new room, they pointed out, was much larger than the old one and even had a walk-in closet. She would easily make friends in Merrick. Besides, they were moving just a few miles west of Wantagh. Her old friends could visit whenever they wanted.

It was about that time a devastating event happened in Amy's life. One day, while her parents were at work, one of her father's acquaintances, who'd been hired to lay new tiles in the bathroom, seduced Amy. She was just twelve years old and knew almost nothing about sex. Guilt-ridden and confused, the young girl kept a terrible secret for a long time.

Yet years later Amy amended the story of what happened that day in Wantagh. She boasted to friends that she'd lost her virginity in the seventh grade; she'd "fucked the tile man." Sex had become a gateway to acceptance.

It was an alarming pattern of altering the truth in order to cope with disappointment and anger. It helped Amy see events in her life as fun and wild rather than crushing and confusing. With Joey Buttafuoco as her mentor, Amy was headed for trouble.

Chapter
Five

In early July 1987, a month before Amy's thirteenth birthday, the Fisher family moved into their new home. That fall Amy enrolled in the eighth grade at Merrick Avenue Junior High.

It wasn't easy being the new kid. Amy was quiet and felt shy around her more boisterous classmates, most of whom had known each other since elementary school. But within a few months Amy had settled in nicely. She even met a classmate, John Psillis, in art class who became her first boyfriend. Amy and John passed love notes surreptitiously in class and met after school for mild make-out sessions. Amy went to his football games and wrestling matches and cheered loudly from the bleachers. At night on the telephone Amy and John talked for hours.

But by the end of the semester the relationship had ended abruptly. John told her he liked another girl in school, and Amy was crushed. A few weeks later she saw him at the junior high school prom with his new girlfriend. Amy remained composed. Wearing a new dress and dabs of makeup, she spent the evening with a coterie of girlfriends, also dateless that night. They took a white limousine home.

Amy enrolled at John F. Kennedy High School in the fall of 1988, shortly after she turned four-.teen. It was her third transfer in three years.

John F. Kennedy came with a reputation. Of the three area high schools—John J. Calhoun in North Merrick, W. C. Mepham in North Bellmore, and John F. Kennedy in South Merrick and South Bellmore, it was Kennedy that was considered the "cool" school, where teenagers drove better cars than their parents; a place where joining a popular clique was tough, but getting dumped from it wasn't.

By age sixteen, when New York teens can apply for a junior license, many Kennedy students begin driving trendy cars, gifts from well-to-do parents. The student parking lot, on the south side of the school, fills each morning with convertibles, Corvettes, and an occasional BMW. To supplement allowances, and to pay for gas and new clothes, some students work at fast-food restaurants and shops on Merrick Road or in Sunrise Mall in nearby Massapequa.

Kennedy students tend to socialize at Saturday night parties held throughout the school year in their South Bellmore and South Merrick neighborhoods. A party hosted by one of the more popular students in school can draw as many as one hundred friends and classmates, with festivities spilling onto the sidewalk until dawn.

Once the weather turns warm, parties move to Tobay, the town beach, or Jones Beach, both one expressway exit off the Wantagh Parkway. For seniors, beach parties are almost a ritual, beginning as soon as school lets out on Friday afternoons. When classes end for the summer, the beach party scene travels out to the oceanfront clubs and bars in Hampton Bays, about an hour east of Merrick.

But not everyone fits neatly into this picture of popularity and acceptance. Amy Fisher didn't. Seldom seen at parties or hanging out in the parking lot after school, Amy Fisher, it seemed, always had somewhere else to be.

"Amy was rarely, if ever, at parties," said Steve, a recent Kennedy graduate. "She kept to herself. Those parties are what get you in. You get to know everyone that way. She didn't seem to care."

She probably did care. But somewhere along the way Amy Fisher realized that being popular in high school took a level of confidence that she did not possess. So she took an alternate route—to capture the spotlight by being different. By the time she was arrested, it was an approach she'd nearly perfected.

In general, Amy didn't share much about her life with schoolmates—except to talk about her older boyfriends. "She always bragged about going out with older guys," a senior noted.

The teenager's flair for fashion and prodigious wardrobe were renowned. Mostly Amy favored comfortable clothes—oversize Champion sweat-shirts, jeans, and red cowboy boots—but she also wore provocative outfits, years before other girls in her grade. In her skimpy shorts and crop tops, Amy Fisher attracted the attention she craved.

Boys at the high school took notice. Amy was petite—five feet three inches, just like her mother—and pretty. The childhood pudginess and glasses were gone, and Amy let her wavy, above-the-shoulder dark hair and bangs grow un-til the locks tumbled down her back. Sometimes she'd pull her hair back in a high ponytail fas-tened with a neon band.

Yet for all her talk of boys and her unbridled promiscuity during senior year, Amy Fisher had only one real relationship: she dated a classmate, Rob, for almost a year. The couple split up shortly after Amy met Joey Buttafuoco but remained bud-dies, still getting together on occasion. In the fall, a few months after Amy's affair with Joey began, they went to the beach. Rob snapped pho-tographs of Amy perched on a sand dune, the ocean behind her.

In high school Amy faced her share of adver-saries as well. In her sophomore year she ran afoul of a particular group of girls at John F. Kennedy. For the most part the friction was con-tained by cutting remarks and an occasional shove in the hallway. But toward the end of the year the tension escalated. One morning in front of the cafeteria, Amy got into a screaming fist-fight with one of the girls in the clique, a senior, bigger than Amy. As a large crowd gathered, the other girl repeatedly punched Amy in the face, breaking her nose and dislocating her jaw. Amy wore braces at the time, and several of her teeth were displaced. She ended up in the hospital, having surgery on her nose. A few days later her entire face turned black and blue and swelled enormously. In great pain, Amy could barely eat for weeks. She missed final exams and was laid up for most of the summer.

The Fishers, extremely upset, filed a $1.2 million negligence lawsuit against the school district, charging that it failed to protect their daughter. The senior was charged with a misdemeanor of assault but eventually pleaded guilty to a violation of harassment in juvenile court. Amy received a permanent order of protection against the girl, and her parents paid the Fishers $5,100. The civil case against the school district, due for pretrial hearings a week after Amy's arrest for attempted murder, has been adjourned until next year.

There were other difficulties for the Fisher family. Several members of their extended family died of breast cancer. In recent years Elliot Fisher had a falling-out with several relatives, and large family gatherings at the holidays ended abruptly.

Perhaps the most unsettling blow occurred in the 1980, when Elliot Fisher's heart condition deteriorated, forcing him to undergo quadruple bypass surgery. His doctors prescribed daily medication and advised him to eliminate stress. Amy's arrest, and all that followed, was so devastating that Elliot Fisher had to skip half of his daughter's court proceedings. And when Amy was in jail, before posting bail, her father rarely felt strong enough to visit.

In many ways Amy's life before Joey seemed unremarkable. She played soccer, jogged around the school track, and fancied herself a Nintendo expert. Keeping up with a childhood passion, she painted in watercolors and talked about studying at the Fashion Institute of Technology in Manhattan.

She watched soap operas—especially "Days of Our Lives"—and downed six-packs of diet sodas, fervently watching her weight. Amy liked to spelled her name "Aimee"—even requesting it read that way in her high school graduation program.

She loved music from the '60s and '70s and often blasted songs by Bread, the Beatles, the Doors, and the Righteous Brothers on her LeBaron CD player. She liked to listen to music at home, too. In her bedroom she hung a skull and bull's horns from the wall. It was one of her favorite decorations.

Unlike some of her girlfriends, Amy wasn't fond of the club scene. Now and then she joined a crowd of friends at Escapes, a dance club in Merrick. Hardly the "wild child," Amy usually positioned herself at the edge of the dance floor, perusing the room. She didn't smoke or drink and never experimented with drugs.

Although the Fishers were not particularly religious, Amy was raised Jewish. She complied with some traditions, telling friends not to call on holidays, when her family did not use the telephone after sunset. In prison, before her bail was posted, Amy requested Kosher food.

The Fishers were a neighborly family, but as a rule they kept to themselves on Berkley Lane. Elliot and Rose Fisher had a small circle of friends and relatives—Amy's grandparents and her mother's younger sister—who visited occasionally. Amy was particularly close to her aunt and treasured a dainty sapphire necklace the older woman had once given her.

When Amy was sixteen, her dad brought home Muffin, a feisty Yorkshire terrier. Although it was understood that Amy would care for the puppy, daily walks often fell to Elliot Fisher. But Amy loved Muffin, dressing her up in pink ribbons and playing with her in the fenced-in backyard. Muffin usually slept in a cage in the upstairs hallway, between Amy's room and her parents'.

Before Amy met Joey, her relationship with her parents consisted of the typical teenage roller coaster of emotions and miscommunication. The chaotic state of her bedroom caused minor squabbles. Amy usually kept the door closed and instructed the family housekeeper to skip it when tidying upstairs. But other, more serious problems developed when Amy was about sixteen. When arguments became heated, Amy occasionally threatened to leave home. Usually she ended the rancor by slamming her bedroom door and calling friends on her private telephone line, talking for hours.

Most of the serious troubles began shortly after that first trip to Joey's repair shop. Amy's relationship with her father, especially, worsened. When the teenager began disappearing for hours in the evenings, Elliot Fisher frequently called his daughter's beeper number to ask where she was and demand she come home.

Amy remained close to her mother. "She used to say 'My mother's like a sister to me,'" recalls Paul, the gym owner. On quiet evenings at home in Merrick, Amy joined her parents at the dinner table and talked about graduation, college, and future plans. She hoped to open a clothing boutique in Massapequa—she even had the exact location picked out. Her parents promised to help her get started. Amy wanted to sell comfortable, stylish clothes.

On Sundays the Fishers' only day off from Stitch 'n Sew, the family usually spent time together. Amy and her mother often shopped, meandering through stores at Sunrise Mall. A few months before her arrest Amy joined her parents on an excursion to a boat show at Nassau Veterans Memorial Coliseum in nearby Hempstead. Arm in arm the family strolled up and down the aisles, scoping out yachts and power boats.

That same winter, during Amy's Christmas vacation from school, the threesome took a cruise for nearly a week to St. Thomas in the Virgin Islands. The Fishers swam and tanned on the beach and shopped during the day. At night they dined in the ship's restaurant and took moonlit walks on the deck. One sunny afternoon they snapped photographs of each other on board the ship, mugging for the camera.

By the time she met Joey Buttafuoco, however, Amy Fisher had developed into a young woman who clearly lacked a sense of self-worth and self-determination. Growing up with few limits and generally getting what she wanted made it hard for Amy to cope with rejection and disappointment. She expected things to go her way. "Her parents didn't set down a lot of rules," a close friend said.

Although she liked to think of herself as much older than her years, in truth Amy Fisher was far more immature than her high school classmates. Desperate for attention, even negative notice, Amy wanted little more than acceptance from her peers. She was a lonely child who grew up to be a lonely young woman, eager to be loved and admired. As the public would eventually learn, this wasn't just any insecure teenager. It was a young girl who acted and reacted on a thin tether of emotion, easily influenced and unable to foresee the consequences of her actions.

"She was ripe to be taken advantage of," said Matthew Rosenblum, one of Amy's lawyers. "There are all sorts of victims walking around out there who wind up becoming defendants. She's one of them."

One of the clearest signs that something was awry with Amy Fisher showed in her report card from John F. Kennedy. An intelligent girl, Amy Fisher brought home grades that were average at best. She had done well in school as a child, but by high school she had stopped working and barely studied for exams, hurriedly copying homework every morning during homeroom or in the minutes before the bell rang for class. As a freshman she registered for Spanish but showed up to class unprepared each day. "The teacher would be telling her to do something and Amy was like, 'Nah, I'm dropping it anyway,' " said a former classmate. "She never did any work."

In her junior year Amy was absent so much that she was forced to attend summer school the following July. By the time she entered her senior year, she managed to arrange her classes—including gym, home economics, government, economics, and English—from periods one to five, the first beginning at 7:35 A.M. Amy was almost always late. She boasted to friends that she woke just minutes before the bell, dressed hastily, and sped the three miles to school.

Amy's last class, English, ended at 11:41 A.M., and from then on she was free to do whatever she wished. Her parents returned from work around 6:00 P.M., and expected Amy home for dinner. But by then the seventeen-year-old had had more than six hours on her own. It was during these long afternoons that Amy Fisher courted trouble.

In many ways life became more dangerous for Amy once she learned to drive. With a license and a new car, there was no keeping her home. She had been eager to drive for years, often practicing in her father's 1987 tan Ford Suburban or her mom's 1982 dark red Cadillac. Shortly after she turned sixteen in August 1990, Amy took her road test and passed. By October she ripped open an envelope from the Department of Motor Vehicles in Albany and found her junior driver's license. Delighted, she immediately began hounding her parents for a car of her own.

It didn't take much pressure. Elliot Fisher sited the Dodge Daytona at a used-car dealership in Merrick. It seemed ideal. Just to be sure it was in good condition, he brought it to Complete Auto Body, four miles from the Fisher home, and asked Joey Buttafuoco to check it out. The repairman test-drove it, examined under the hood, and gave Elliot Fisher a thumbs-up sign. A few days later Elliot Fisher bought the car and gave the keys to Amy.

A short time later, just before Christmas 1990, Elliot Fisher took the family Cadillac to the body shop for repairs. This time Elliot Fisher took Amy along. He would regret that decision for the rest of his life.

Chapter
Six

Joey Buttafuoco stepped out from behind his desk as Elliot Fisher entered the office of Complete Auto Body. The two men shook hands and turned to watch the slight, dark-haired young girl walk in, the door closing gently behind her.

"Here comes the little princess now," Elliot Fisher said with a wry smile. He introduced his only child to Joe Buttafuoco.

The two men, chatting cordially, discussed the work needed on the Cadillac. Amy wandered around the office, reading inscriptions on Joey's trophies and plaques. She said little. She seemed shy, reserved. As he computed an estimate, Joey couldn't help but notice her. Amy was sixteen—just a few years older than his son. That fact must not have crossed his mind.

Amy was not impressed by the repairman. She later told a friend she thought Joey was fat. But in the next few months Amy began to feel differently. She visited the shop several times. She wanted the car personalized with pink stripes and the name "Aimee" written on the driver's door. Not long after her first meeting with Joey, Amy had a minor accident with the Dodge, damaging the driver's side mirror. The teenager panicked. Her parents had warned her not to use the car after school, and Amy had disobeyed. She called Joey for help. From then on, Amy and Joey saw each other frequently.

Joe Buttafuoco alleges that Amy kept reappearing at Complete Auto Body because she crashed her car as many as ten times purposely, just to have an excuse to see him. Amy and her family insist there was only one other accident—the following August. But they insist that something else was going on at Complete Auto Body: that Joey and the shop's adjustors filed large insurance claims for nonexistent repairs. Joey, meanwhile, says Elliot and Rose Fisher paid Complete Auto Body almost $14,000 in repairs. Amy has told a friend that is a lie. When Amy had an accident with the Dodge three days after her seventeenth birthday, she told a friend that Joey reported to insurance agents that the car had been totaled, even though it wasn't.

Shortly after the shooting, rumors surfaced that the Nassau Police Department believed Complete Auto Body was a chop shop and had even put a wiretap on the telephone lines. Joey and his father, Caspar, adamantly deny allegations of wrongdoing at the repair shop.

Whatever, if anything, was going on in the accounting department of Complete Auto Body, something portentous was happening between Amy and Joey. They were becoming pals. They flirted and teased each other. They bantered lightly about sex. Joey says Amy talked about a variety of young men, wanting him to believe she was promiscuous. Amy, he added, wanted to believe he was promiscuous as well.

Amy had always been attracted to older men. Even when she first began high school, Amy all but ignored the pubescent boys in her classes. "As soon as we got into the ninth grade, right away Amy was looking at eleventh-grade guys," one classmate had said.

But this wasn't a high school senior or even a recent graduate. This was something entirely different—a thirty-four-year-old married father of two. A casual friend of her father's. A man old enough to *be* her father.

In the months that followed her first visit to Complete Auto Body, Amy made no secret of her interest in Joe. Wearing her trademark flimsy outfits, she struck an alluring image in the mind of the repairman. She became a familiar sight at the shop after school. She got to know Joey's dad, Caspar, his brother, Bobby, and all the mechanics in the garage. One afternoon Joey bought her a slice of pizza and a diet cola while another mechanic worked on the Dodge. He began taking her along when he ran errands for the shop.

That winter was a troubled time for Amy at home. She cut school a few times and started hanging out with friends in nearby Levittown until late. Her parents tried to enforce a curfew, but Amy paid no attention. Now that she had a car and a junior license, she was out of the house more than ever. After three weeks of constant arguing, one evening in early February Amy bolted. She drove to her aunt's house and spent the night, without telling her parents where she'd gone.

The Fishers, frantic, called the police and filed a missing persons report. Over the phone a weary Elliot Fisher described his only child as "totally uncontrollable." The police officer jotted it down in his report.

They were words that Elliot Fisher would later wish he had never uttered. At Amy's arraignment for the attempted murder of Mary Jo Buttafuoco a little more than a year later, Assistant District Attorney Fred Klein pointed to that missing persons report as proof that Amy Fisher was beyond the control of anyone. Klein quoted from it extensively, much to the dismay of Amy's parents.

"Her own parents can't control her," Klein said. "How are they going to get her to court? She is completely beyond the control of her parents, of the school, and of this court." Waving the missing persons report as affirmation, Klein described Amy as a former runaway who had dropped out of school, a defiant teenager with a dangerous streak.

It wasn't exactly accurate. Following that February night at her aunt's house, Amy had moved in with her grandmother for two weeks. It wasn't an ideal situation, but her parents felt it gave the family a chance to cool off. Elliot and Rose were relieved to know where their daughter was. They knew Amy's grandmother would take could good care of her.

Still, it was an unhappy time for the Fishers. At one point during those two weeks, Joey Buttafuoco says that Elliot Fisher dropped by the auto body shop to commiserate about his daughter's wild ways.

Once Amy returned home, things improved, but just slightly. She began going back to school regularly. In March she was absent only twice. But every morning her first-period teacher marked her late. She ended up failing a class.

Around that time Amy Fisher posed for her senior class photograph, even though she was still in her junior year. By custom John F. Kennedy begins its preparation for senior yearbooks more than a year ahead.

Amy perched on a stool against a light blue background. The photographer counted to three, and Amy smiled. An attractive image: a young girl in a white print sweater, her hair parted on the side. She wears a touch of dark pink lipstick and around her neck the sapphire necklace she treasures. A portrait of Amy Elizabeth Fisher. One year later that photograph made the front page of all three New York City dailies and the cover of *People* magazine. Headlines blared the scandal she had created. Amy Fisher. The wild child. A case of teenage fatal attraction.

By spring of 1991, a few months after meeting Joey Buttafuoco, Amy began talking about moving out for good. A classmate, Chris Drellos, planned to rent a house with a few buddies. Amy asked if she, too, could move in and even gave Drellos money as a down payment. She and Drellos began dating casually. Although she liked him, Amy knew whom she really wanted.

On July 2, 1991, she got her wish.

That afternoon Amy dropped off the Dodge at Complete Auto Body, and Joey offered to drive her home. The ride from Baldwin to Merrick is quick—about ten minutes. Joey was gone for almost three hours.

After months of flirting, teasing, and innuendo, Joey made his move. He had sex with sixteen-year-old Amy Fisher in her parents' house—in Amy's light grey bedroom with stuffed animals lining the dresser.

Later that evening, around 8:30 P.M., Joey and Amy met again, this time at the Freeport Motor Inn and Boatel, a tidy, sixty-one-room motel just a mile south of Elliot and Rose Fisher's Stitch 'n Sew. At the front desk Joey asked the desk clerk for the short-stay rate—four hours—and paid the bill, $45.36, in cash. Amy waited in the car parked in back.

"Room 256," said the clerk, Paul Fischer, handing Joey the key. "It's on the second floor, around the back. It has a king-size bed."

"Thanks," said Joey, reaching for the door. "See you later."

Joey and Amy climbed the back stairs arm in arm. Joey unlocked the door, and Amy stepped into room 256. It was a bright, airy room, with a blue-and-white bedspread and nautical pictures on the walls. The door closed behind them, locking automatically. As Joey pulled Amy into his arms, the sixteen-year-old felt a fervor of unfamiliar feelings.

The relationship stayed steamy. After July 2 Joey and Amy began meeting almost daily at the Fisher home, in south shore motels, or in an upstairs apartment at Complete Auto Body after the shop closed for the day. They frequented the Gateway Motel in Merrick and returned to the Freeport Motor Inn four more times: the last time in March, just two months before Amy's arrest. The couple usually met after 5 P.M., when Joey finished work for the day.

Two of the motel's managers remember Joey from his visits. He chatted amiably as he filled out his registration card and always paid in cash. Apparently Joey didn't worry about getting caught. He printed his real name on the registration cards.

Still, Joey wasn't completely blasé about his after-work activities. He gave his business address—1025 Merrick Road—rather than One Adam Road West.

At the Freeport motel one evening, Joey, impatient, sighed when Paul Fischer pulled out the registration card.

"Fill it out for me, will you?" he asked.

The manager complied. Later the young man faced a flurry of questions from private investigators and police who wanted to know why the handwriting on the card was different. Fischer

shrugged as he recalled the exchange with Joey.
"He asked me to do it—he was a regular, so I did,"
he said. "I looked it up in the files after I saw him
on TV, when he was out there saying he never
cheated on his wife. I spelled it wrong, but it was
there—Buttafuoco. It was definitely him."

The motel's day clerk, Jim, met Joey once over
the summer, shortly after the auto repairman's
first tryst with Amy. Joey arrived alone, paid for
the short-stay rate, and then hung around for
almost an hour, waiting.

"He didn't seem mad," recalled Jim. "He was
very friendly, nice to talk to. Then he saw her and
said, 'See you later,' and went around back. Most
of the men come in alone. The women don't flaunt
themselves when they come in for a four-hour
stay."

The next time Jim saw Joey Buttafuoco was on
the evening news almost a year later. Sitting at
home in his living room, Jim did a double take. I
know this guy, he thought to himself. How do I
know this guy?

The name Buttafuoco was so familiar. Buttafuoco. Jim listened carefully as Joey repeatedly
said, "Absolutely not," whenever he was asked
about a sexual relationship with Amy. Suddenly
Jim remembered. He began to laugh.

Chapter
Seven

During the first weeks of her affair with Joey, Amy attended summer school, making up credits for a class from the semester before. At the end of July she landed a sales clerk position at Jean Country in Sunrise Mall in Massapequa, but she only lasted a few weeks. Although she was well liked by other employees, management wasn't pleased by her performance. Amy frequently called in sick and showed up late. By August she was gone.

Far more important things were going on in her life. She and Joey often met for sex on his new thirty-one-foot power boat, *Double Trouble*, then took a spin around the bay, not far from the Buttafuoco home. Once they raced past the south shore home of John Gotti, Jr. Joey waved to the Godfather's son. John Gotti, Jr., waved back.

Amy would later recount that Joey and Amy occasionally motored west to a popular Island Park beach bar, Paddy McGee's, for happy hour on the outside deck. Bartenders vividly recall Joey's *Double Trouble* pulling up to the dock, McGee's Landing, but add they don't specifically recall the Merrick teenager on board.

He was apparently untroubled about being seen with Amy. Amy's friends witnessed the pair hugging and kissing. Sometimes friends gave Amy rides to motels or the repair shop to meet Joe. When Joe worked at the shop, Amy occasionally went by herself to the marina, tanning on the deck of *Double Trouble*.

Amy quickly fell in love. Joey made her feel special. He listened to her. He made her laugh. Amy told him everything—about her old boyfriend, Rob, her dislike for school, and how she couldn't identify with any of her classmates. She didn't think she needed school. What good would it ever do her? She told him how her parents didn't understand her.

Joey did. He knew what she wanted, what she needed. Again and again he told her he loved her. He stroked her hair and told her how beautiful she was, how sexy and special she made him feel.

Amy was proud to be seen with the repairman. Everyone, it seemed, knew him. Six feet, 235 pounds, burly and strong, he was gregarious and dynamic.

He spent money on her—taking her out for expensive candlelit Italian dinners, buying her clothes and jewelry. Always Joey's wallet bulged with wads of cash. Money impressed Amy. A lot.

In March, just two months before the shooting, Joey gave Amy the notorious white COMPLETE

Auto Body T-shirt. Amy slipped it on over her clothes. It hung almost to her knees. She was delighted. She began wearing it to school, talking about her boyfriend, the auto mechanic.

"He took a young girl and introduced her to an adult world, a sexually active world," said an auto repairman who knew Amy. "She was a young girl with low self-esteem, didn't think much of herself, didn't love herself. Then along comes this thirty-six-year-old guy who preys on her weak points. He brings her to a level she's never seen before. She's feeling great. Joe filled the voids and gaps in her life. He promised her a bed of roses. She used to say that: 'He promised me a bed of roses.' He painted a real rosy picture."

It wasn't all rosy. Amy got upset when it seemed all Joey wanted to do was have sex. She fretted that it was all he cared about. At times her temper flared and she didn't phone him back right away when he called her beeper number. She complained about him to her friends and talked about breaking up. But Joey always knew how to make it up to her. He'd kiss and cajole. He'd send her flowers.

For the high school senior, flowers and pronouncements of love made the difference. Joey almost always sent Amy roses, although once he bought her an arrangement of spring flowers in a clay pot. Joey was careful. He bypassed neighborhood florists who might know the Buttafuoco name and instead used the Island Flower Shop in Island Park several towns away. According to Amy's friends, Joey didn't use his credit card.

Joey also avoided sending the flowers to Amy's house, where her parents might answer the door and ask questions. Instead he instructed the florist to bring them to the North Bellmore home of Amy's friend, Maria Murabito, a diminutive, blond-haired girl Amy met the same summer she began seeing Joey.

Maria and several of Amy's other friends weren't impressed by Amy's married lover. In fact, they didn't like him at all. Now and then a friend gingerly suggested Amy find someone else. Amy brushed off their concerns with a laugh.

Joey was experienced, she told them, he knew just what to do. Besides, she'd often add, breaking into giggles, "he fixes my cars. He loves me. And we have great sex."

Recalling Amy, Maria Murabito was sad. "He kept telling her 'I love you.' All her real friends love her. Now she's caught up in this big-time mess because of this goon."

"She'd say 'I luuuuv Joey' in a joking way," another friend added. "But I'm sure deep down she really loved him because she wanted it so bad to be true that he loved her. She said he told her he was leaving his wife. I think she really, truly believed he would."

Amy's parents were not oblivious of what was going on in front of them. Sadly, though, they believed Joe and Amy when both vehemently denied a sexual relationship.

In early August, about six weeks after the affair

began, Amy's mother took her to a gynecologist.
The young girl had been complaining of painful
irritation. The doctor gave a startling diagnosis:
a mild case of chlamydia. Amy, flustered, told her
parents she'd gotten it from Joey Buttafuoco.

Elliot Fisher was incensed. He called an assistant district attorney James Clark, and said his
daughter might be having an affair with a married man. He was thinking of pressing charges
of statutory rape. Clark told Amy's father his
options: he could file a complaint or contact the
local police precinct. The DA's office says that
Elliot Fisher told them he couldn't bring his
daughter in to file charges. In her shaky emotional state, he said, he was afraid he would lose
her.

Meanwhile, Amy went to the repair shop and
told Joey. She said her parents were very upset
and had called the police. The repairman panicked. He immediately called the Fisher home. He
told Amy's mother he wanted to come over that
night and explain.

A few hours later, Joe Buttafuoco stood in the
Fishers' living room and insisted nothing, abso-
lutely nothing, was going on between him and
Amy.

In the beginning, Elliot Fisher was suspicious.

"You better not be going near my daughter," he
said, his voice deadly quiet.

Joey was convincing. "Mr. Fisher, I would
never . . . your daughter, she's just sixteen. I'm a
married man, with two children. A beautiful wife.
How could you think I'd even dream of touching

your daughter?" She's infatuated that's all. Do you realize what this would do to me if anything like this got out?' "

In front of her parents, Amy recanted. She said she had lied. It hadn't been Joey after all. Elliot and Rose, embarrassed, apologized to the repairman.

But as he left the Fisher home that evening, Amy would later claim Joey could barely contain his mirth. He winked at Amy and gave her a poke in the ribs. "How'd I do?" he said softly.

Amy tried not to laugh. "You almost convinced me."

Later Amy recounted the entire story to Paul, the gym owner. She repeatedly joked about it over the next few months. "He BS'ed my father so bad," she told him. "It was so funny."

Joey tells a different version. He says that Amy showed up at the shop saying she'd told her parents he'd given her the disease, believing he would cover for her. "I said, 'What do you mean, cover for you? What is that supposed to mean?' " I went to Mr. Fisher and I said, 'There's no way I'm involved.' I told him, 'I was never involved with her on that kind of a level.' I was totally disgusted."

Over time, all the deception and secrecy shrouding the affair proved bewildering for Amy Fisher, clouding her vision of reality and make-believe. As flippant as she tried to be about her relationship with Joe, the confusing messages he sent her were taking its toll. She convinced herself that she and Joey were co-conspirators in this flamboyant life-style they led: their torrid fling: wild spending sprees; high-priced prostitution. Amy bragged that Joey said he could help her get a job as a nude dancer at Goldfinger's, a strip bar in Queens. Amy claimed he'd told her he had connections: she could earn up to $500 a night.

Amy Fisher relished the excitement, the risk, the danger. Somehow her secret life with Joey Buttafuoco held it all together. "Amy always used to say 'Joe is the best liar around, and I learned from him,' " says Paul.

They'd managed to fool everyone. It was only when Joey began to pull away that Amy realized Joey had been fooling her, too.

From the beginning of the affair, Amy envisioned a future with the repairman. There was one problem: Mary Jo.

She was hard to escape. Joe talked about her frequently, and photographs of Mary Jo, her arms around the kids, hung prominently at Complete Auto Body.

Amy was extremely jealous of her lover's wife. On one of her first visits to the repair shop, she surveyed the pictures of Mary Jo carefully.

"Is that your wife?" she asked, trying to sound indifferent. "She's very pretty."

Joey Buttafuoco seemed to enjoy Amy's jealousy. He needled her relentlessly by praising Mary Jo. "She's very beautiful," he'd say. "I happen to have a very beautiful wife."

A few months before the shooting, Amy was

61

hanging out with Paul in the gym. She began to gripe about Joey. "He's always saying how beautiful his wife is," Amy complained. "I hate that."

"I bumped into them the other day," Paul told her. "At a restaurant."

"Do you think Mrs. Buttafuoco is pretty?"

"She's very pretty."

"Prettier than me?"

"Amy, she's a thirty-something-year-old woman. You're a seventeen-year-old girl. It's different."

Amy was not satisfied. It wasn't the first time she'd cross-examined a friend about Mary Jo Buttafuoco. Some months earlier she'd managed to get a photograph of a younger Mary Jo and showed it to Stephen Sleeman. The exchange was familiar.

"What do you think, honestly?" Amy asked. "Who is better looking?"

"You," Sleeman responded without hesitation. "Definitely you."

"Who has a better body?"

"You do."

"You really think so?"

"I really do."

No amount of reassurance helped. Amy constantly compared herself with Mary Jo. She spoke often of Joey, how much she wanted their relationship to last. She told Sleeman that Joey told her that Mary Jo had found out about two affairs he'd had in the past. One more, his wife had warned, and the marriage was over. Amy began to talk hopefully about the dissolution of the Buttafuoco marriage.

"She'd say 'Just imagine if I get married to Joey someday. Think how great everything's going to be. I'll be set for life,' " recalled Sleeman. "She wanted Joey so much. It never stopped—Joey, Joey, Joey, it's all she talked about. She couldn't understand why Mary Jo had him when she was so crazy about him."

Some of Amy's confusion is understandable. The messages she picked up from Joey were exasperatingly mixed. He told her he cared for his wife. Mary Jo had been his childhood sweetheart—he could never do anything to hurt her. But at the same time, Joey made it clear that Amy had a special place in his heart—he loved her deeply. If it weren't for Mary Jo, he told her on many occasions, he might well be with her. And if something ever happened to Mary Jo, well, he could probably get along quite nicely without her.

In the early months of her relationship with Joey, Amy must have believed that Joey wanted his wife gone—that the casual talk of "what if something happened to Mary Jo" was his unspoken message to her. Amy was convinced that she and Joey had a special language. They were partners. Amy trusted the relationship with her life.

As Amy would later recount, she had been so confident of Joey's love that in early December, about five months after that first afternoon tryst at her parents' home, Amy Fisher gave the repairman an ultimatum: she told him to divorce Mary Jo, or else their affair was over.

Joey's reaction stunned the teenager. He flatly told her he didn't think they should continue to see each other. Later, Amy told Paul she simply couldn't believe it. For months, Amy bragged, Joey had professed love for her. She somehow believed he would leave his wife.

For a few days, Joey and Amy didn't speak. Then Amy began to call him, upset. She regretted her demand, and wanted to make up. But the Merrick teenager soon realized the damage had been done. Joey had backed off. He began to tell her that with Christmas approaching he needed to spend more time with his kids. From then on, Amy told Paul, she and Joey fought constantly.

Joey considered breaking off the affair entirely, but he didn't. Sex with the pretty high school senior was exhilarating. Amy made him feel young. He liked it that she often told him how great he was in bed. Once he boasted to an employee at the auto body shop that he'd given Amy her first orgasm, and that was why she'd flipped for him.

They continued to have sex throughout that winter and into the spring. But everything had changed. Joey called less frequently and seemed aloof at times. Amy heard the rumors, never substantiated, that Joey had someone new—another dark-haired sixteen-year-old. Amy said she didn't care. "Joey likes young girls," she told Paul with a shrug.

Amy did care. A lot. The hurt of being discarded stung. Even though by now she'd met Paul at the gym, and talked about having fallen in love with him, Amy Fisher was destroyed by Joey's rebuff, and shocked her ultimatum had backfired. Just two weeks before the shooting she told Paul she was stupid for believing all of Joey's lies. "I don't know why I ever believed all that stuff about 'if it weren't for Mary Jo it would be me,' " she said. "It would never be me. All that flattery was fake. Why did I ever believe him?"

At the same time Amy had begun hanging out in Brooklyn on the weekends. One of her best friends was dating a guy who belonged to a gang. Amy was fascinated by talk of turf and gang loyalty. She was impressed that many of the young men had guns. She talked about the excitement of their world, how they "rubbed out" their rivals.

Amy Fisher had a rival: the woman who had it all. Joey's beautiful wife, Mary Jo.

A source who knew both Joey and Amy puts it this way: "When Joe heard his wife got shot, he knew immediately what happened. I am sure he sat there, put his head down, and said, 'I can't believe she did it. Me and my big mouth.' Joe planted the seed. He didn't want it to happen. But he planted the seed."

A year later, sitting in a six-by-eight jail cell, Amy Fisher heard through her attorney how Joe Buttafuoco characterized their relationship. "I in no way had a prearranged meeting with Amy Fisher," he said. Once, he explained, he bumped into Amy at a Freeport pizzeria halfway between his auto body shop and her parents' upholstery store. "I was in the place picking up some lunch, and she happened to have been there." Twice he saw her at Paddy McGee's. "She came walking in, but was quickly ushered out because she was underage."

And yes, he did give her the white COMPLETE AUTO BODY T-shirt. "I gave her the T-shirt because she was such a good customer—she made our top ten hit list," he said. "And that's all it was."

The affair touched a nerve deep within Amy. In a time of great disorder, Joey Buttafuoco became her strength. His reassurance that they were a wild and audacious pair, that lies and trickery were somehow good—as long as you weren't caught—left Amy confused. Lessons of moral values and hard work—the ones her parents had tried to impart—were forgotten. Joey's ruinous teachings stuck.

"Amy said Joey used to tell her, 'Forget about what's right and wrong—do whatever you feel.' " says Paul. "He'd say, 'If you enjoy doing it, do it.' "

In many ways the summer the affair began signaled the first serious signs that Amy's life was spiraling out of control. Her parents sensed something was wrong, but the teenager was skilled at lying about where she'd been, what she'd been doing. Elliot and Rose Fisher wanted to believe nothing terrible was amiss, and they did.

But six days a week, as the couple labored at

Stitch 'n Sew, their daughter was running wild. It was that summer that Amy Fisher began to map out a pernicious plan to get rid of Mary Jo Buttafuoco.

It was the same time that the teenager stepped into a seedy, destructive new role—working as a prostitute.

Chapter
Eight

How and why Amy began working for ABBA escort service is still uncertain, but the timing of her involvement in prostitution is curious. By the end of the summer, less than six weeks after beginning the affair with Joey Buttafuoco, Amy Fisher was soliciting clients for money. It was just before her seventeenth birthday.

In the fall, when Amy began her senior year, her classmates noticed something new: she wore a beeper at all times that periodically went off during classes. The beeper itself wasn't novel among John F. Kennedy students. Many of the young people carried them to keep in touch with friends. It was yet another status symbol in the affluent Long Island towns of Bellmore and Merrick.

In Amy's case the beeper had a more lurid purpose. For her classmates it was the most provocative gossip they had ever heard in the halls and gym classes at John F. Kennedy High School:

Amy Fisher worked for an escort service, and those beeps in English and economics class were from clients, calling to set up appointments for sex.

Working for ABBA escort service made Amy feel more adult than her classmates. That it was a shocking and forbidden trade made it all the more compelling. Amy yearned for attention from older men. As a prostitute, she got it. In the facade she created, her clients made her feel desirable and loved. The other, more horrifying feelings, she pressed down deep. On the surface, being a prostitute didn't feel sleazy at all: it seemed almost glamorous. Once more, Amy's attention-grabbing ways had arisen—only this time in a far more precarious arena.

On at least one occasion, Amy bragged about the job in a girls bathroom at school. Sex, she told her fascinated listeners, was fun, and the money from the escort service was great. Besides, she often added, she got bored easily and needed a lot of sex, with different partners.

Amy's involvement in prostitution didn't look very glamorous when it inflamed the front pages of the New York City tabloids a little more than a week after her arrest. Her covert life-style was dissected and displayed to millions. Her parents ached with each new disclosure. Their daughter's terrible secret had become about as public as it could get.

The conflagration began when Peter De Rosa, a short, chunky twenty-nine-year-old salesman from Levittown, Long Island, picked up a newspaper and noticed a photograph of Amy being escorted by court officers to jail, her long hair hiding her face. He skimmed the article, fascinated. Amy Fisher. He couldn't believe his luck. Not only did he know her, but he knew a way to make a lot of money. Fast.

De Rosa reached for the phone and called Fox network's "A Current Affair," the weekly television scandal sheet. De Rosa had a titillating deal to negotiate: a homemade videotape of him having sex with Amy Fisher. He told producers his story: he had been an ABBA customer, one of Amy Fisher's clients. On three occasions he had paid for sex with Amy. If the price was right, he'd sell the proof.

Producers at "A Current Affair" were elated. This was a coup of infinite proportions. The murderous high school call girl at work. A ratings victory, to be sure.

After some haggling, De Rosa and the show's representatives agreed on a price: $8,000. It would include a brief interview, on camera, with De Rosa speaking from the shadows. De Rosa signed a contract, very pleased with himself. That feeling would be short-lived.

Cameras rolling, De Rosa told Steve Dunleavy, the managing editor of "A Current Affair," that he called the ABBA escort service in March and paid for three dates with Amy while she was on Easter recess from school. An ABBA intermediary had told him that a girl named Stacey would meet him at his Levittown home. When Amy arrived, however, she told him her real name.

71

Identified on the show, appropriately, as "John," De Rosa said he paid Amy $185 for their first sexual encounter. She then told him to call her directly in the future, and the fee would be less. He did. Their second tryst cost him $100; their third, $150.

It was the second date that De Rosa filmed, stealthily setting up the camera in his bedroom closet. He claimed he filmed the fourteen-minute, thirty-six-second tape as a gag. On it, Amy is pictured sitting on the edge of his bed as De Rosa helps pull off her jeans. Clad only in a skimpy white unitard, Amy giggles, lies back, and criss-crosses her legs. She bounces up and then falls back again as De Rosa sheds his boxer shorts.

He joins her in bed between the mismatched linens, and the camera catches several minutes of their arms and legs flailing. Amy is heard asking De Rosa to turn out the light, and he does, reaching for a lamp switch on the nightstand next to a bottle of baby oil. For the next seven minutes there is darkness. In the background are muffled strains of Aerosmith's "Back in the Saddle Again" from the CD player. At one point Amy is heard to say, "That's great, lover."

A few days before it aired the tape, "A Current Affair" sent a camera crew to Amy's high school. Dunleavy explained that he wanted to ensure the girl on the tape was indeed Amy Fisher. On the street, out of sight of school officials, the reporter played brief portions of the film to six seniors who knew Amy from various classes. Seconds after the girl on the screen emerged and bounced on the side of the bed, the students called out in a chorus, "It's Amy, that's Amy."

On Sunday afternoon, the day before it broadcast the sizzling Amy Fisher segment, "A Current Affair" contacted the New York City tabloids, eager to drum up publicity for their broadcast. The show's publicists aired a tantalizing excerpt of the video to reporters and offered an abridged transcript of Amy's conversation with her john.

The promotion maneuver worked perfectly. The next morning New York City tabloids ran front-page stories, hyping "A Current Affair." LOLITA TAPES, screeched the *Daily News*. HIGH SCHOOL STUDENT BY DAY, CALL GIRL BY NIGHT, blared the *Post*. MAN: FISHER "SHY" IN SEX ENCOUNTER, boomed *New York Newsday*.

Amy's chat with De Rosa, before and after the lights went out, was garbled and faint. It didn't matter. Her words, written on the bottom of television screens nationwide, played to a fascinated audience.

AMY: (Let's) take care of business, then we don't worry about this when we take care of pleasure. I don't like to think of business and pleasure all at the same time.

DE ROSA: Ahh, I think I know what you're saying.

There is muffled conversation about a horror movie, about his CD collection and her CD player in the Chrysler LeBaron.

AMY: Are you going to take off your T-shirt or are you going to leave it on?

DE ROSA: I don't know—you want it on?

AMY: Take it off.

They talk about scratches on his back. He says they are from his cat.

The lights go out. When they are back on, he asks her to come to a bachelor party he is planning to throw for a friend.

DE ROSA: What if I'm going to have a bachelor party for my friend? Do you think you could go?

AMY: Anything. I'm wild. I don't care. I like sex.

DE ROSA: You would be by yourself, you wouldn't have a friend?

AMY: Oh, no. Nobody knows I do this.

There is some talk about kinky, S&M sex.

AMY: Oh, I wouldn't sit and let a whole bunch of guys slap me around. I would never do that. If you paid me two thousand dollars, I would not do that. I can't do that. . . .

DE ROSA: I'm just saying for my friend.

AMY: Oh, no way. Uh-uh. Forget about it.

DE ROSA: That's why . . . I said you and your friend come and your friend would do it.

AMY: No. My friends don't know that I do this.

DE ROSA: Then you could hang out with me.

AMY: Well, thanks.

At one point there is some discussion that sounds like Amy is talking about Joey Buttafuoco.

AMY: He's an older guy. He just turned thirty-eight.

DE ROSA: He's still married? . . . He has kids?

A telephone rings, and they go out the door.

Then De Rosa comes back into the room and turns off the camera.

On "A Current Affair," De Rosa talked briefly about Amy. "Well, I guess she was not your average hooker," he said. "She didn't wear makeup. She was quiet . . . she seemed kind of shy, but at the same time she was easy to talk to but definitely not the type of girl you would expect to be a call girl. . . . I paid her, and we proceeded to have sex. She spoke about going into business and how she wanted to make a lot of money. She would do anything for a nickel."

De Rosa added that he last spoke to Amy on May 18, the day before Mary Jo Buttafuoco was shot. He had called Amy on her beeper, wanting to set up another date. Amy turned him down. She said she was having her period. Two weeks later their sexual encounter played for millions nationwide.

For Peter De Rosa, selling the tape would subsequently seem a drastic error in judgment. Within a week of the "Current Affair" broadcast, his name leaked and ran in the New York City dailies. Film crews immediately pulled up to the modest Levittown house he rented with two friends. A technician began panning the camera around the house, taking in the modest boat in the driveway, the beer bottles strewn on the kitchen table visible through the front window. Camera still rolling, a reporter knocked loudly. De Rosa peaked through the curtain and withdrew, aghast. "No, no, no," he said nervously, waving his hands. He disappeared upstairs.

As soon as the press crew left, De Rosa hurried to his car and sped off. He didn't return until almost midnight.

His next-door neighbor, an older man, watched the events unfurl from his front lawn. The man was puzzled. He'd heard something buzzing along Marksman Lane. Something about a tape, about that chubby kid Peter next door. Something about Amy Fisher? Was that it? The man wasn't sure what was going on. All he knew was that lately the house next door was quiet, much more so than usual. No loud music blasting through the windows. No raucous laughter and bands of young people in and out at all hours. Indeed, the house next door had been awfully quiet lately.

The tide of reporters did not abate. They drove up at all hours, knocking on the door, wanting to know more—more about Amy and ABBA. Within days of the press descent on the little house in Levittown, De Rosa's roommates, disgusted, told him to move out.

What seemed like an amusing hoax at first had become a humiliation. A very public one. At last the graying man next door learned what Peter De Rosa had done.

"Well," he said, putting down his garden tools, "I don't think much of the guy, that's for sure. If he did a shitty thing like that . . . he's got to be a little perverted."

De Rosa may have had second thoughts about

what he did, but "A Current Affair" didn't. The "Lolita tapes" were a brushfire success, earning the show high ratings.

Yet its broadcast did not go off without a glitch. Just before "A Current Affair" aired the tape, rival "Hard Copy" snatched portions of the video off a satellite feed. "Hard Copy" then ran one minute and fifty seconds of the sex scenes throughout its late afternoon telecasts, scooping "A Current Affair."

"Hard Copy" rushed to defend its tactics, proclaiming the film snippets "fair use." The producer of "A Current Affair" lashed out, saying fair use for a news broadcast of a competitor's story would last at most five seconds and would credit the competitor. "Hard Copy" had not only failed to give the show credit, it had actually enlarged the video to rid the TV picture of the "Current Affair" logo.

Fox Television, parent of "A Current Affair," announced it would sue Paramount Pictures TV (parent of "Hard Copy"), for up to $1 million. Hoping to avoid the suit, "Hard Copy" apologized publicly, trying to smooth ruffled egos.

But Steve Dunleavy wasn't mollified. The managing editor of "A Current Affair" grumbled as he read the morning's newspapers. The *New York Post* reported that "Hard Copy" had "picked up" the video from a satellite feed. Dunleavy slammed down the paper and reached for his office telephone. He got a *Post* staffer at once.

" 'Picked up'?" he barked. "That's like saying Willie Sutton withdrew money from banks. It was *stolen.* But then I've always said impoverished midgets make the best pickpockets."

Such is the nature of warfare when the dispute is over the blistering tale of seventeen-year-old Amy Fisher.

Chapter Nine

ABBA escort service operates from the ground floor of a two-story wooden gray house on Grand Avenue in Baldwin, just three-quarters of a mile from Complete Auto Body. Behind its red door is a strange, almost mystical sight. The front parlor, small and somber, is decorated with a dozen or more antique wig stands and furnished with Victorian-style couches and overstuffed chairs. Busts of hairless female mannequins sit eerily on the windowsills and shelves, peering vacuously into the room. A life-size doll of a male figure, clad in red-and-white-striped pants, a suit jacket, and an ascot, is positioned on one of the couches, its hands resting on its knee. A few cats jump up next to the figure of the man, settling down for an afternoon nap.

From this room a graying, heavyset fifty-six-year-old woman, Lorraine Wurzburg, first dispatched Amy Fisher to men willing to pay almost $200 an hour to fulfill their carnal desires.

For almost a decade, Wurzburg, who calls herself Rita, has rented the sexual services of young women without remorse. She herself was once one of them, a prostitute in New York City. In the early 1980s Wurzburg got her start working for a pimp at his Queens-based escort service, answering telephones at night and setting up assignments. She quit a few years later, and in late 1984 Wurzburg opened her own service and named it Allure.

Wurzburg was not known as a compassionate boss. When one young prostitute walked out on a client after refusing to perform a specific sex act, Wurzburg began screaming at the girl over the phone, demanding money. Another time a prostitute called to complain that a customer refused to wear a condom. Wurzburg snapped, "Well, you are the one who is going to lose out on the money."

Although Allure was a thinly veiled prostitution ring, Wurzburg kept her business low-key and managed to avoid arrest for several years. On November 29, 1990, her luck ran out. She sent two women and a driver to a job booked by an undercover vice squad detective. The three were arrested, and the following day police raided Wurzburg's apartment, seizing business records and $18,000 in cash. Wurzburg was arrested and charged with promoting prostitution. In jail, she met for the first time one of the prostitutes, a twenty-four-year-old aspiring dancer from Queens, who had been working for her for several months and knew her only as Rita.

Not long after she was jailed Wurzburg posted her own bail money—$20,000—in cash.

On February 8, 1991, Wurzburg pleaded guilty to the charges against her and paid a fine. She also was forced to forfeit the $18,000 nabbed by police.

But just days later she was back in business, this time under a new name: ABBA. One of her drivers even called the young prostitute who had been arrested the previous November. "He said that Rita said a lot of the regulars missed me," she said. "He said, 'We are opening up in a place in Queens. C'mon back.' I was shocked."

ABBA didn't open in Queens. It was listed in the Nassau County Yellow Pages, with a Brooklyn-Queens area code and a Nassau County address. Its phones rang in Wurzburg's Grand Avenue apartment in Baldwin, around the corner from a police station.

Wurzburg admits she once ran a prostitution ring but insists ABBA is different. Her business offers female companionship only for dinner and dancing and no longer provides sex. "I am legitimate," she says. "I already paid my dues."

But police and ABBA employees say otherwise. Since she opened ABBA, Wurzburg has employed as many as two dozen women at a time, who provide sex for anywhere from $85 to $300. A cagey businesswoman, Wurzburg ran her company well. Each woman ordinarily turned over about $1,000 weekly, netting Wurzburg upward of $20,000 a week, most of it tax free.

Wurzburg recruited employees by word of

mouth and from advertisements placed in sex magazines. The young women were screened by a driver, who supposedly checked to ensure they were over eighteen.

Amy Fisher, just sixteen years old, didn't have much trouble dodging the age requirement. She produced a fake identification card, claiming she was twenty-one years old, and used an Italian last name as an alias. It could not have been difficult to realize the teenager was lying. Anyone who looks at Amy Fisher would probably guess her to be about fourteen or fifteen years old.

It didn't matter at ABBA. Young, pretty, white: in no time Amy Fisher would be in great demand. She was given a beeper and ABBA's direct telephone line. She began work almost immediately.

The day the "Current Affair" tape aired, reporters descended on ABBA with verve. A slovenly Wurzburg, clad in a rumpled housecoat and worn slippers, at first denied hiring Amy. Standing in her doorway, she screamed at journalists, demanding they leave. ABBA, she asserted, was no longer in business. "It's all closed up and gone," she shouted. "Go away! I don't know an Amy Fisher!"

A Jeep filled with teenagers slowed down as it passed the Grand Avenue house. The young people crammed in back broke into cheers. "Amy, Amy, Amy," they yelled.

Nearby, neighbors watched the spectacle, nonplussed. There had always been an oddness about 2569 Grand Avenue. They never saw anyone going in or out. Never saw the residents mowing the vast lawn, taking out the trash, or sweeping the walk.

"It was strange how no one ever answered the door when the kids went trick-or-treating there," noted a man who lived a few doors away. "I guess it's not so strange after all."

The standoff between reporters and the eccentric Wurzburg was tense. When pressed about Amy Fisher, Wurzburg broke down and said she couldn't deny hiring the girl. But just as suddenly she snapped, "Did Amy send you? Are you implying we had something to do with the shooting? We don't hire teenagers, we never have, we never will. We only hire women over thirty-five."

Amy Fisher, half that age, proved otherwise. In her first few months at ABBA Amy built a base of about ten steady customers, older professionals, including doctors and lawyers, from the south shore of Long Island. After she totaled her Dodge Daytona in August, she asked friends to drive her to jobs. Chris Drellos took her to the houses of at least three clients, waiting for her in his car. In the fall, Amy saw men after school. A few times Stephen Sleeman drove her to ABBA to pick up her fee.

Amy charged about $180. Customers paid her with an ordinary credit card, signing a voucher made out to a florist. Amy then dropped off the voucher in a mailbox at ABBA and picked up an envelope of cash—usually about 30 to 40 percent of the job, or around $100.

"She would have a slip like a merchant, but it was made out to some florist as the payee," said a source. "The johns paid, and it was being funneled through a florist."

Interestingly, shortly after Amy's connection to ABBA became public, a Long Island florist repeatedly called an attorney representing one of the principals in the case, seeking legal counsel. When reporters heard the tip and called the florist, asking what, if anything, was his connection to the case, the owner thundered, "We don't know anything!" and slammed down the phone.

By the winter of 1992 Amy Fisher no longer worked for ABBA. She had devised a more lucrative way to earn money. As she had done with De Rosa, she told clients to call her directly. The men were pleased. They saved money. Amy, too, was satisfied. She earned more.

Amy's scheme to shaft the escort service backfired. At her bail hearing following her arrest, the prosecutor, Assistant District Attorney Fred Klein, argued that it proved Amy was duplicitous. "This is hardly a typical high school student," he said. "She's not even your typical prostitute. . . . She is so shrewd and so manipulative and so brazen that she has attempted even to cut out the escort service from giving them money; by the use of wearing a beeper that she wears to school and wears out of school, she has had her customers contact her directly and pay her directly, and she has kept the money. This is the type of defendant that you are dealing with, Your Honor."

Missing from Klein's discourse was any suggestion of how or why Amy Fisher became a prostitute. For the Nassau County District Attorney's Office, answering that question is apparently not a high priority. The office maintains that Amy Fisher discovered ABBA on her own, probably noticing its advertisement in tiny print on the back pages of the *Village Voice*. Nassau County police probing the case against Amy say they did investigate Joey Buttafuoco and found no evidence that he was tied to ABBA.

Some believe the district attorney and police aren't looking very closely. In a conversation with Paul, Amy claimed that Joey introduced her to ABBA. She isn't the only one levelling similar charges. One source close to the case insists that the repairman peddled drugs to prostitutes and johns in the mid 1980s.

"Buttafuoco was a low-level drug dealer for years," the source said. "This guy is definitely dirty. He supplied drugs to prostitutes and johns. Not a good boy. Amy comes along, and here goes this little fly into the web. To say this sixteen-year-old got into prostitution herself is utterly ridiculous."

Others have made similar allegations. Owners of a rival escort service and a young woman who says she used to buy cocaine from Joey appeared on "9 Broadcast Plaza," a local television talk show. The escort service associates said that Joey was a driver and canvasser for ABBA, transporting young women to their assignments and luring new recruits. The sources, in disguise, their backs to the camera, said the girls knew Joey Buttafuoco as Jo-Jo.

"What Joey was doing for Rita at ABBA or Allure, or whatever she's calling it now—he was a canvasser for her," said the source, called Mel on the show. "He used to find girls for her. He was a driver and a canvasser. He'd go out and try to lure girls into working for this profession."

Mel said he and his partner, called George on the show, first heard of Joey Buttafuoco in the winter of 1991, when they learned that Joey was luring some of their employees to work for ABBA. Joey, they said, gave ABBA's telephone number to several of their girls and a driver in a Queens diner. The employees then turned over the phone number to Mel and George.

Mel said he called Rita at ABBA and complained. "We told her in a nice way, 'Why don't you do business properly?'" he said. "'Don't do this.' She agreed, very amicably, not to do it. Two weeks or a month later, same thing happens again. Same guy."

Mel said he instructed the girls to beep him immediately if they were ever approached by Joey again. They did. Late one night Mel, George, and a few other men confronted Joey in the diner.

"We warned him not to do this, and to do business in a proper way," Mel said. "He was very amicable—he's a very good talker, a very good weasler."

Joey, Mel said, was well-known among prostitutes on the south shore. He said Joey was an unpopular driver among the girls at ABBA because he often demanded sex—and didn't pay.

"He would tap the faucet with the girls," he

said. "The girls didn't want to work this way. They don't want to be bothered by a driver. . . . He had a reputation for that."

Mel added that it didn't surprise him that evidence tying Joey to ABBA was difficult to uncover. "People in this industry—the girls, the drivers, the owners—do not want to come forward," he said. "He's banking on that. He is banking on that."

A separate source interviewed by a reporter for the *New York Daily News* claimed that parents had complained that Joey attempted to recruit young girls in front of a high school.

Lisa, a woman in her early thirties, who also appeared on "9 Broadcast Plaza" in disguise, said she used to buy cocaine from Joey in 1985, when he and Mary Jo lived in Baldwin.

"When we wanted cocaine, we could get it from Joe—for a price," she said. "I would say anybody who knew Joe knew they could buy from Joe."

Mary Jo, she said, was present during their business transactions. "She knew all about it," Lisa said.

The *Daily News* also reported that Long Island prostitutes and johns nicknamed the repairman "Joey Coco Pops."

Eric Naiburg, Amy's lawyer, is Joey Buttafuoco's most vocal accuser, shooting salvos at every opportunity. "Mr. Buttafuoco is the pimp who put Amy in the damn business," he frequently told reporters. "He's a pimp and a liar. He struts the world like a Teflon titan, thinking he's untouchable. I beg to disagree."

Joey Buttafuoco denies all the charges. He says he never heard of ABBA escort service, and Amy never said a word to him about prostitution. "I didn't know she was a whore," he said.

He admits he spent twenty-eight days in a rehabilitation clinic for cocaine addiction but says he has been drug free since 1988. He scoffs at the accusation that he sells drugs.

Some of the allegations against Joey have already been shot down. In their haste to unearth proof of Joey's connection to ABBA, two television networks aired erroneous reports in the first weeks following the shooting. On one show the anchor reported that ABBA's utility bills were routinely sent to Joey's home. Another news broadcast pronounced that ABBA's telephone rang at Complete Auto Body. Both charges, investigated by Nassau County detectives, proved false.

Police have been reported as saying that none of the allegations made by the associates of the rival escort service were brought to them.

But clearly there is evidence to examine and sources to question. Eric Naiburg has repeatedly called for the district attorney to indict Joey Buttafuoco for statutory rape. In early July Naiburg even offered a juicy cachet: he would allow Amy to testify against Joey before a grand jury.

The prosecution, however, wanted to keep the case clear and unmuddled. Shortly after Naiburg called for Joey's indictment, the DA turned it down, saying there wasn't enough evidence to prosecute.

A detective who interviewed both Joey and Amy put it this way: "That guy's an asshole. But come on. Do you know what would happen if we locked up every guy who made love to a sixteen-year-old?"

If Joey Buttafuoco was involved, whether as a business associate of ABBA's or simply in encouraging Amy to be a hooker, it wouldn't surprise those who observed his relationship with the girl.

"She would do anything he told her to do," said a friend who knew them both. "He had absolute power over her. He was basically her first lover. She talked about that one kid in high school, but Joe was really it. All that stuff about a million other guys—that was later, once she got started with the escort service and all. That was after she started up with Joe."

Chapter
Ten

Even amid the most passionate moments of his affair with Amy Fisher, Joey Buttafuoco had no plans to end his marriage. He had a nice life on Adam Road West. Mary Jo, pretty and attentive, was always there for him.

She listened to his daily report about goings-on at Complete Auto Body and got along well with his family—Joey's parents, brother, and two sisters. If he was late or fabricated an excuse about helping a customer at the shop, she didn't ask questions. Mary Jo was a good mother, kept a meticulous house, and cooked savory meals every night. Lounging at the beach club, her sunglasses pushed up against her bleached-blond hair, Mary Jo cut an attractive figure.

The couple met when Joey was fourteen and Mary Jo fifteen, both freshmen at Massapequa High School on Merrick Road. Joey was instantly smitten by the hazel-eyed Mary Josephine Connery, daughter of a large Irish-Catholic family from nearby Massapequa Park.

Joey and Mary Jo were an item almost at once. Mary Jo attended his weight-lifting and arm-wrestling matches and bragged about his victories to her friends. The couple spent many hours cuddling as they watched television at each other's houses and hanging out at Complete Auto Body with their friends.

Mary Jo's parents, Francis and Pat Connery, were pleased. Joey's family was close-knit and Italian-Catholic. Like the Connerys, the Buttafuocos were natives of Massapequa, moving into their two-story brick home on Biltmore Boulevard when Joey was just three years old.

While Mary Jo was the oldest of several girls, Joey was the youngest of the Buttafuoco clan. His mother, Louise, sisters, and brother, Bobby, fussed over him. But tragedy struck the family. Soon after moving into the new house on Biltmore Boulevard, Louise Buttafuoco died. Joey was barely four years old.

His father remarried. His new wife, Willie Mae, had a son, Bruce, from a previous marriage. A Brooklyn native, Caspar Buttafuoco had been a race-car driver and mechanic, working at tracks all over Long Island. Willie Mae promoted car races in Freeport and Islip. After they married, Caspar Buttafuoco owned several gas stations in Jamaica, Queens, and then, with a partner, opened Complete Auto Body and Fender on Merrick Road in Baldwin. It was 1970, the same year

Joey and Mary Jo met. In a short time the business prospered.

When Mary Jo was in her sophomore year at Massapequa High, her family moved a few miles away, to a large, rambling blue Victorian-style house in the village of Massapequa Park. Surrounded by a brown picket fence, the house, larger than Joey's, has a small garden in the back and a wooden country-style sign hanging by the front door: The Connery House. Behind the painted shutters, pretty Mary Jo Connery began to make wedding plans.

There seemed to be little doubt about the future. Joey's devotion to Mary Jo was unmistakable. In their high school yearbook in 1974, he didn't list any credits. Instead he requested the words under his photograph say exactly what was in his heart: "I love Mary Jo." Nothing and no one, it seemed, could keep these two apart.

Yet the courtship endured turbulent times. At some point during high school Amy has told friends that Joey revealed he got a girl pregnant. The girl refused to have an abortion, and eventually gave birth to a son. The boy, now 19, lives with his mother in Florida.

Amy says Joey seldom sees his son. She claims that the repairman often gripes about the child support payments he has made over the years.

There is no independent corroboration, and, through his attorney, Joey has refused to comment on the charge.

Shortly after high school graduation, Joey joined his brother, Bobby, working at Complete

Auto Body, learning to fix all models of cars. Earlier that year Caspar Buttafuoco had bought an adjoining property and expanded the repair shop almost twofold.

Joey already knew a considerable amount about repairs—he'd been tinkering in the shop throughout his adolescence. But now, as a member of the team, the young man took his role more seriously. Gradually Caspar Buttafuoco would give his son more responsibility, teaching them how to run the business.

Joseph Buttafuoco and Mary Josephine Connery were married in 1977 at St. Rose of Lima Roman Catholic Church, where priests would fifteen years later say prayers for Mary Jo. The wedding marshaled a joyful assortment of friends and family. Guests marveled at the young couple—Joey was twenty-one, Mary Jo twenty-two,—as they drifted on the dance floor. A family member toasted the union and said a prayer for God's blessing. On that euphoric day no one could have imagined that the couple's future held a daunting event: that a troubled teenager would eventually shatter their lives with a .25-caliber bullet.

The newlyweds moved into their first home—a modest little place on Ashland Avenue in Baldwin, just a five-minute drive from the shop. Their son, Paul, was born three years later and three years after that, a daughter, Jessica. In many ways Joey and Mary Jo had just what they had expected from their lives. Their little house was warm and inviting. Paul's and Jessica's toys were scattered in the nursery, and Catholic statuettes stood on display in various rooms. One year, shortly after they married, Joey splurged and bought a motorcycle. He loved tearing around the streets of Baldwin. The couple also ordered special license plates for their cars—for Mary Jo, MJB; for Joey, CAB, for Complete Auto Body.

But behind the closed doors of 637 Ashland, a problem was intensifying and getting out of hand. Joey was snorting cocaine. It started as a sporadic treat late at night after the kids were put to bed. But Joey had hooked up with a local Long Island rock-and-roll band, doing drugs with the musicians.

In 1986 the Buttafuocos sold their house in Baldwin and moved on to One Adam Road West in the upscale neighborhood of Biltmore Shores in Massapequa. Their new house cost $186,000; the couple took on a $126,000 mortgage. Financially they were set. Like his father and older brother at Complete Auto Body, Joey would eventually earn a six-figure income.

Some years earlier Joey and Bobby had pooled their earnings and bought out their father's partner. But by the mid–1980s the brothers' business relationship was crumbling. Joey's drug use was out of control. Caspar and Bobby were upset. After months of bitter arguing, they told him his drug use was not only destroying his life, it was damaging the reputation of the business they'd worked so hard to build.

Not long after moving to Massapequa, Joey sold back his share of Complete Auto Body to his father and brother. Michael Rindenow drafted an agreement and drew up the legal papers. The parting was cordial. Joey believed he was better off on his own. With the money he received, he opened his own auto body shop nearby, on Newbridge Road.

But within two months the business collapsed, and Joey lost tens of thousands of dollars. Broken, the repairman at last faced his problem. He checked into South Oaks Mental Health Center in Massapequa for its twenty-eight-day drug rehabilitation program.

With the help of counselors and fellow addicts, Joey studied the twelve-step program and mastered its tenets—to live one day at a time and surrender his addiction to a higher power. He fought hard. He stopped drinking alcohol. He resolved to turn his life around.

It took time. Even after he completed the program and had begun to attend daily meetings, Joey wasn't always sure he could stay clean. But he treasured the constant love and support of his family. Their fortitude made him struggle all the more. And there was Mary Jo, eternally in his corner. Her strength gave him hope.

Since the fall of 1988 Joey has managed to stay clean, never once relapsing after completing the rehab program. He went back to work at Complete Auto Body, only this time as an employee, not a part owner. Joey is now a supervisor, with two foremen, as well as his father and brother, above him.

As he took control of his life again, Joey's energies refocused. He joined Future Physique a few miles from his home and began to work out several times a week. Paul became Joey's personal trainer.

In the spring of 1990 Joey discovered another splendid new outlet: boating. He bought a twenty-one-foot runabout, docking it at the Biltmore Shores marina next door. The following summer he brought home *Double Trouble,* the thirty-one-foot Cigarette power boat he would later use for trysts with Amy Fisher. The name of his new boat delighted Joey's friends and neighbors. *Double Trouble.* It suited the mischievous Joey Buttafuoco perfectly.

Boating became the Buttafuoco family's passion. With Paul and Jessica in tow, Joey and Mary Jo motored out of the marina, waving to other boaters, and pointed *Double Trouble* out to sea, eager to explore new areas. In the evenings they rallied friends and relatives and took quick jaunts up Massapequa's Grand Canal into South Oyster Bay. Almost every Sunday Joey stopped by Richie's Quality Meats on Merrick Road and bought flank steaks to grill on board the boat. The butchers, Mike and Chris Ferretti, looked forward to his visits. None of their customers were as colorful as Joey. "He comes in here and says, 'Let me have a happenin' flank steak. Make sure it's a happenin' one,' " said the twenty-five-year-old Mike Ferretti, grinning. "Nobody else asks for that. He kids around with you. Really funny guy."

Paul and Jessica especially enjoyed family outings on *Double Trouble.* From their dad they learned important lessons about water safety. Best of all, he taught them to water-ski. Little Jessica so loved the water that Joey nicknamed her "Jet Ski." Sipping soda at the beach club's refreshment stand, Joey watched his kids swimming in the bay, splashing with the other children, overflowing with giggles. When they competed at local swim meets, Joey was always there to cheer them on. Paul and Jessica, he liked to say, were real water rats.

Mary Jo and Joey were content on Adam Road West. It was a quiet street, filled with lots of young couples who had lived in Massapequa their whole lives. Many, like Joey, sent their children to the same public schools they had once attended. Neighbors were friendly and warm. Trading gossip at the beach club was an everyday event.

The Buttafuocos were by far one of the most popular families in the area, their home a favorite meeting place for the neighborhood kids. Joey, always cheerful and buoyant, could be counted on to help fix a flat or join in an informal soccer game. He was just as helpful to neighbors—the first to call if a car required a jump start or furniture needed moving.

Mary Jo was equally well liked. Quiet and more reserved than her husband, she developed her own circle of friends, meeting at the club and in each other's kitchens. An attentive mother, she carefully supervised Paul's and Jessica's homework every evening and proudly taped their report cards to the refrigerator.

At Biltmore Shores Beach Club parties every summer, Joey and Mary Jo headed conga lines and danced the cha-cha. On holidays, they joined their families at mass at St. Rose of Lima about a mile away. Almost every month, it seemed, a family event brought their extended family together—a communion or birthday, an anniversary or graduation. Joey, Mary Jo, and the kids never missed a celebration, driving over to visit with his parents or hers.

If the marriage was rocky, few could tell. Joey and Mary Jo seldom seemed to argue. When they did, it was usually about trifling matters, taking out the trash and mowing the lawn. Mary Jo did almost all the housework and now and then, aggravated, pushed Joey to do his share.

Always affectionate in public, Joey and Mary Jo sunbathed side by side on the deck above their garage and shopped together at the markets along Merrick Road. Holding hands, they'd wave to Ross, the hairstylist, and Mike and Chris at the butcher shop. When Joey stopped by the stationery store Friday nights for his weekly lotto ticket, he often joked to friends that he and Mary Jo were headed for the Bahamas with their winnings.

"He'll say 'Mary Jo and I are outta here, and we're taking you and your brother with us,'" said Mike Feretti, the butcher. "Joey's always talking about his wife. They look like two happy people."

It's a sentiment echoed by many in Biltmore Shores. Mary Jo and Joey, an ebullient couple with lovely children. No one suspected anything was amiss. Joey had covered his tracks deftly.

Yet in those last few months of the repairman's relationship with Amy Fisher, portentous things had happened at One Adam Road West. Just after Thanksgiving shots were fired into the living room, and in February two Molotov cocktail-type devices were found burning in the street in front of the house. Both times Mary Jo called the police. It was frightening. Even more, it was bizarre. Police have not determined whether Amy Fisher was behind these incidents, but detectives investigating the case believe she was.

The weekend before she was shot, Mary Jo celebrated her thirty-seventh birthday, surrounded by family and friends. Joey, by her side, gave her a big hug and a kiss and smiled when she blew out the candles.

For him, the arrangement was working out fine.

Chapter Eleven

In the months before the shooting, an important person entered Amy Fisher's life: Paul, the gym owner.

They met in January, just a few weeks after Joey told Amy he needed to spend more time with his family and less time with her. About that time Joey suggested that Amy join Future Physique. On and off for more than two years, Joey had done the training circuit several times a week. He wasn't a dedicated bodybuilder, but he was in good shape and tried to maintain muscle tone.

Joey told Amy about Paul. He was a terrific personal trainer, Joey said. Amy should look him up.

Amy took his advice: she signed up at the gym, paying the annual $179 fee in cash. On her first visit she left a note for Paul, asking for an appointment. A few days later they met for a training session.

"She was swinging on the bars like a little monkey," Paul recalled with a laugh.

From their first meeting, Amy and Paul clicked. Despite their twelve-year age difference, they quickly became buddies. Once again the teenager had found an older man to make her feel special.

This one, fortunately, was unmarried. Paul was good-looking, too—light brown hair and mustache and gentle blue eyes. He'd been a bodybuilder since his early teens and continued to work out strenuously every day.

Within a short time Paul and Amy were like old friends. Paul often teased her, saying she was so much like him when he was seventeen.

"You think you've got everything under control—you think you know it all," he'd tell her, laughing. "I can see right through you. You're a little conniving devil."

With Paul as her personal trainer, Amy began working out several afternoons a week. At night she returned, hanging out after the gym closed at 10:00 P.M, perched behind Paul's desk in the office and sipping Carbo Force, an energy drink. On many occasions Amy talked about Joey.

She said she and Joey had split up but were still friends. Amy wanted to stay on good terms, in case she ever needed work on her car. Now and then she mentioned that she'd had dinner with the repairman. She always added that they didn't have sex. All the physical stuff, Amy insisted, had stopped.

Paul just grinned. "I know you're lying," he'd say.

"Really, I'm not," she answered. "We just had dinner. He wanted to, but I said no."

Amy wasn't saying no. She was still seeing Joey, meeting him in motels all over the south shore of

Long Island. It was a confusing time. She knew she was losing Joey, yet the repairman still beeped her, wanting to get together for sex. She told friends that he continued to tell her how beautiful and sexy she was. And he never stopped saying that he loved her. Only Mary Jo, she claimed he told her, stood in their way.

At the same time, Amy developed a crush on Paul. The gym owner told her he cared for her but wanted their friendship to develop slowly. He kept reminding her that she was just a kid even though she might feel grown-up.

Amy clung to her new friend. In Paul she'd found a confidant, a special companion. Yet she wasn't always honest with him. She often fudged stories about her past and lied outright about what was going on in her life.

Paul usually saw through her deception. He knew she was still involved with Joey, regardless of how many times she'd insisted it was over. But he suspected there were other, more formidable secrets. He knew there was a side to Amy Fisher he simply hadn't reached.

Paul began to question Amy about details that confused him. Why did she always have so much money? He knew she didn't have an afterschool job. Or did she?

One evening, on a whim, Paul guessed. He told her he'd heard rumors she worked for some kind of escort service. The gym owner instantly knew he'd struck a nerve. Amy looked uncomfortable.

"Who told you that?" she asked.

Paul randomly mentioned the name of a friend from the gym.

Amy hesitated. "If I tell you the truth, you won't want to see me anymore," she said.

"That's not true," Paul insisted. "What's the deal?"

Amy tried to explain. "I went on a few dates, just dinner, with these older guys," she said in a rush. "I didn't do anything. One of the guys said I reminded him of his daughter. You don't have to have sex, you know."

Paul doubted her story. "Amy, don't you have respect for yourself?" he said sternly. "You shouldn't be doing things like that. You've got some good ideas about business, about what you want. Go to school and finish up. That's the direction you need to go in."

"Everyone screws up sometimes," Amy replied, shrugging.

Within a short time, Amy confessed to Paul that she had fallen in love with him. Paul reminded her that he wanted to keep the relationship casual and uncomplicated. He gently suggested that she not visit the gym every night.

Amy kept up the pressure. She began buying him lunch when she dropped by the gym in the afternoons and occasionally picked up little gifts. Once she found a list of compact discs Paul wanted to buy. Amy surprised him and bought all of them the next day. When Paul needed a new transmission for his 1981 aqua-turquoise Corvette, Amy insisted on loaning him $1,400.

"You don't have to buy me things," Paul often said.

"I know," Amy said. "I want to."

She wrote him a long letter, telling him she had never felt so close to anyone before meeting him. On Valentine's Day she sent him three cards. Once she made an audio tape. On it, she talked about her growing attachment to him. Her favorite seventies songs played in the background.

Amy's interest in Paul did not sit well with Joey Buttafuoco. He seemed jealous, and Amy was delighted. Even though Joey had just paid for another year's membership at Future Physique, once Amy joined, the repairman never returned. He spent $300 to join another gym—Tommy Tewillger's Maximum in Bellmore.

"Joe is really jealous of you," Amy told Paul. "It bothers him a lot that I hang out with you. He didn't want me to tell you anything about me and him."

On the nights Amy visited Paul at the gym, Joey frequently called her beeper, waiting by a pay phone for her to call back. Sometimes Paul noticed Joey's number: 007 on Amy's beeper. One night when Amy's beeper went off repeatedly, Paul looked again: 007 had called at least three times. He gave Amy a playful poke.

"Man, he calls you a lot," he said. "And you're not still seeing him . . . Yeah, right. I know you think you have me fooled, but you don't."

One night as Paul locked up the gym, Amy turned to him thoughtfully. "Do you believe someone can love someone and still have sex with someone else?," she asked.

Paul shook his head. "No," he responded. "That person probably didn't really love the other person."

Before long Amy and Paul began having sex. Sometimes the gym owner dropped by her parents' house in the afternoons, when Amy got home from school. Usually they waited until the gym had closed for the night.

Many times their amorous evenings were interrupted by phone calls from Amy's father. He was not happy about the relationship between this twenty-nine-year-old man and his seventeen-year-old daughter.

"What are you doing there?" Elliot Fisher would ask Amy. "The gym is closed."

"We're just talking."

"Come home."

Once, after an argument with her parents, Amy threatened to move out. Paul had been talking about relocating to Texas, she said, and she was going to go with him. Elliot Fisher called the gym owner the next day.

"I'll have you arrested," he warned.

"Look," Paul said, exasperated. "First of all, it's Arizona, not Texas. Second, I have no intention of taking Amy. Just relax."

One Sunday, just two months before the shooting, Paul took Amy to his cottage in Vermont. They took a long walk, hand in hand. He told her he would teach her to water-ski in the summer. Next winter they would go snow skiing.

Paul was beginning to feel a growing attachment to Amy. He didn't always trust her and wasn't sure what secrets she still held. But she was pretty and upbeat and full of love. "You've probably had a weird past," he told her. "If you're looking to drop all that and move on, maybe there'll be something for us."

Amy seemed happy. For all her "wild child image," she often sounded like an old-fashioned girl.

"If you wanted to move here, I'd go with you tomorrow," she told Paul, gazing at the mountains. "I would be so happy just sitting with you in the living room watching television."

She told him her fondest dream. "I want to have kids," she said. "I don't want to wait until I'm thirty."

Paul complicates the "fatal attraction" theory. If Amy was obsessed with Joey, why did she fall in love with Paul? If she loved Paul, why did she attack a completely innocent woman?

Amy Fisher was desperate: for love, attention, acceptance. Her friendship with Paul, sadly, could not replace the anguish and bitterness of the past year. It may have helped to fill a void, but it was not enough.

Too much had happened to Amy, and she no longer had any sense of who she was: Elliot and Rose's little girl; Joey's mistress; Peter De Rosa's call girl; Paul's girlfriend. It was too bewildering, too unreal.

Shooting Mary Jo Buttafuoco became the apogee of a year-long odyssey of lies, deception, and emotional abuse. Although Amy initially believed Joey wanted her to kill his wife, the teenager eventually realized that it didn't matter: she and Joey would never be together. All of Joey's hints about their future had been a lie; all the unctuous flattery, phony. Amy was left bitter. She wanted to hurt Joey just as he'd hurt her.

Amy Fisher displaced all that anger onto a blameless woman. For so many months the seventeen-year-old had struggled to understand why Mary Jo Buttafuoco had it all: a beautiful house by the water, a boat, two lovely children. And Joey. No matter how many times Amy had felt Joey's arms around her, and heard his protestations of love, the young girl finally learned the truth. It was Mary Jo who had Joey . . . and always would.

Even as Amy told her tale on the stoop that morning, Joey still slithered away free and clear. Mary Jo had not believed Amy's accusation.

There, right in front of her: Joey's beautiful Mary Jo. The woman who lived the exact life that Amy Fisher craved. When Mary Jo dismissed Amy's charge, it was the final rejection. With a .25-caliber bullet, Amy Fisher tried to expel the demons in her soul.

Chapter Twelve

When two Nassau County detectives closed the door to a small room at police headquarters in Mineola, Long Island, Amy Fisher hunched over on a chair, silent and defiant. Her heart was racing, but she couldn't let them know she was scared.

For the next twelve hours the detectives pressed the young girl tenaciously for her version of what happened on the stoop of Mary Jo Buttafuoco's home. The story emerged in pieces, fraught with contradictions. "She went back and forth," one detective said later. "At times she was very scared and crying. Other times she tried to be a hard-ass. She's a seventeen-year-old who got in way, way over her head."

At one point Amy tried to convince detectives that Joey Buttafuoco gave her a gun in January and told her to kill his wife. "He gave me a twenty-five-caliber handgun," Amy said. "He said he would fix me up with a guy who would get me some bullets."

The detectives, dubious, continued to pump her for more details. Where had he given her the gun? What exactly did he say? Abruptly, Amy recanted. Someone else, a young man named Peter, had furnished the gun. Joey wasn't involved after all.

Amy told the police little about Peter Guagenti. Fact was, she hardly knew him. She had met him only a week before when she and a few girlfriends had piled into her LeBaron and driven to Brooklyn. One of the girls wanted to visit her boyfriend, who lived in Bensonhurst. The group then strolled over to a Greek festival at a nearby church.

Under the elevated subway line on Eighty-sixth Street, Amy was introduced to Peter Guagenti, a part-time auto repair salesman who dreamed of being a doctor. They talked in hushed tones. She told him she wanted a gun; she'd pay him $800. There was some talk of sex, but that, Amy said, was not part of the deal. Peter accepted the offer, hoping his association with Amy Fisher would lead to bed. Instead it led to his arrest.

Early on Tuesday, May 19, Peter Guagenti called Amy's beeper and punched in his phone number. She called back at once. Peter told her he had the gun, a semiautomatic .25-caliber Titan. They agreed to meet at the Fisher home at 11:00 A.M. Amy gave him directions to Berkley Lane in Merrick and hung up the phone.

Amy drove her LeBaron to school. Once in the

building, she grabbed hold of a classmate, Josh, and asked him to take her for a drive. Josh didn't need much convincing. It was a clear spring morning, just six weeks from graduation. The perfect time to cut class.

He and Amy slipped out of school and headed for his car. Amy suggested a route: down Merrick Road a few miles, then turn right on Bayview Avenue. She knew a pretty section by the water. As the friends cruised down Adam Road West, Josh checked out the boats docked in the Biltmore Shores marina. He never realized his passenger was scoping out the corner house next door, preparing for a deadly mission.

Mary Jo Buttafuoco's Oldsmobile sat in the driveway. The front door stood ajar, allowing the morning breeze to waft through the house. On the back deck, the housewife painted lawn furniture.

Amy suggested they return to school. Josh made a U-turn and headed back to Bellmore. Everything was moving according to plan.

Back at John F. Kennedy, Josh returned to class. Amy Fisher did not. She went directly to the nurse's office on the main floor. She didn't feel well, she explained. She needed to go home.

Following procedure, the nurse called Amy's parents at Stitch 'n Sew for permission. Rose Fisher, concerned, asked what was wrong. When told Amy felt mildly ill and needed rest, she gave her consent. The nurse gave Amy a pass to leave the building.

Peter Guagenti was already waiting in front of

the Fisher home when Amy turned down Berkley Lane. She pulled into the driveway, got out, and climbed into the Thunderbird. Amy peeled off $800 jammed in her pants pocket. Guagenti handed her the gun.

Fascinated, Amy fingered the gun on her lap. She gave Peter directions: north to Merrick Road, turn right, then straight about six miles to Massapequa. A right turn on Bayview Avenue and on to Adam Road West. It was a route she knew well.

Amy must have wondered how Mary Jo would react to news of her husband's affair. Surely the woman would feel thoroughly betrayed. Amy wanted to see her adversary stand before her, motionless and bruised, unable to cope with the numbing disclosure. Joey's beautiful wife.

Throughout the grilling by police, Amy Fisher always insisted the shooting of Mary Jo Buttafuoco was an accident. Detectives were frustrated. After hours of probing, they locked her in a holding cell. A short time later they tried again. Questions flew with renewed punch. Why did she have a loaded handgun if she hadn't meant to use it? Didn't she really want Mary Jo Buttafuoco out of the way for good?

Amy couldn't be shaken. She'd only meant to hit Mary Jo. The gun had fired by accident.

In the end, detectives emerged from their night-long interrogation of Amy Fisher with a ten-page handwritten statement. Excerpts were promptly leaked to the press. "I showed her the shirt Joey had given me," Amy had said. "I felt she didn't believe me, and she kept asking me questions, like where I lived, who I was with. At this time I felt she was dismissing me and didn't care about what I was saying. I saw her turn to go back in the house, at which time I took the gun out of my pocket and hit her on the back of her head. I saw her stumble. I had my finger on the trigger. I went to hit her again because I was so angry. I then raised the gun again, and it went off. I heard a pop sound and saw blood coming out of her head."

Police were satisfied with her confession. They led an exhausted Amy Fisher to a holding cell and locked her in. It was early Friday morning. In front of the Nassau County Police Headquarters, Franklin Avenue was already choked with traffic as workers hurried to their jobs in nearby county office buildings. Amy lay down on a cot and closed her eyes. Nothing had turned out the way she'd planned.

A few miles away Elliot and Rose Fisher were frantic. Except for that terrible night a year earlier, when Amy had not called from her aunt's home, their daughter had routinely checked in when she knew she'd be late. But on this endless night hours had passed, and nothing. Amy's mother anxiously peered out the living room window, waiting for the familiar black LeBaron to pull into the driveway.

Rose and Elliot did not sleep at all that night. Every few hours Elliot called the police, only to hang up, frustrated. He wanted officers to canvass the streets of Merrick and Long Beach, where Amy had said she would be jogging. Officers listened patiently and advised him to wait a few hours. Amy, he was reminded, had run away in the past. Give it some time. He would probably hear from her soon.

At 5 A.M., not long before the first rays of sun streaked the sky over nearby Baldwin Creek, Elliot Fisher filed a missing persons report. It struck a haunting, familiar memory of that other terrible night of waiting. This night, however, was even worse: there had been no argument, no problem, with Amy. Several times in the last two days she had complained of feeling ill, but she had appeared to be feeling better. She had ambled out of the house that evening seemingly fine. Her disappearance could not be explained by anything other than a horrible accident.

By now Elliot and Rose hoped the police would take their fears seriously, but once again a sympathetic voice on the other end of the phone told them to be patient and try not to worry.

Around 6:30 A.M. Elliot Fisher drove to Future Physique. The gym had just opened. A few die-hards were already lifting weights in the back.

Elliot Fisher approached the front desk, tired and drawn from worry.

"I'm looking for Paul," he said.

"He works the night shift," the manager said. "He's home."

"Listen, it's very important. My daughter is missing."

The manager dialed the number. The phone

woke Paul with a start. He tried to clear his head. He'd fallen asleep only a few hours earlier.

The manager turned his back and spoke quietly into the phone. "Paul, Amy's father is looking for her," he said. "You want me to tell him to take off?"

"No, no. Put him on," Paul said.

The manager passed the phone across the desk. Elliot Fisher grabbed it.

"Paul, Amy didn't come home last night. Is she with you?

"Mr. Fisher, she's not with me," Paul said. "I haven't talked to her in a couple of days."

"Paul, please," Elliot Fisher said, his voice beginning to break. "Why won't you help me? Why don't you tell me? She must be with you. She always returns my beeps. We think she's dead if she's not with you."

"Mr. Fisher, I'm being truthful with you. She isn't here."

"God, Paul, she's got to be dead. Her mother is petrified right now."

"I know she wasn't feeling well the other day."

"She seemed to be better. She said she was going jogging in Long Beach."

There was a brief pause.

"I'm sure she's okay," Paul said, beginning to worry himself. "If I hear anything, I'll let you know right away. I'll call you in a few hours to see if you've found her. If you haven't, I'll help you look for her."

"Thanks, Paul." Elliot Fisher hung up the phone.

Elliot Fisher headed home. His wife met him at the door, red-eyed and silent. Before he spoke, she knew he'd learned nothing about their daughter's whereabouts.

At 9:00 A.M. the Fishers were sitting in their kitchen, where they had been all night. The phone rang; Rose grabbed it on the first ring.

"You'd better get a lawyer," said Detective Daniel Severin. "Your daughter is being held in connection with the attempted murder of Mary Jo Buttafuoco."

Chapter
Thirteen

Police took Amy's mug shot. Hair pushed back, she looked at the camera wide-eyed and bleak, the graphic image testimony to her shock over what she'd done and its result. Detectives confiscated her beeper, cut a few strands of her hair for testing, and took an ink impression of her feet. Amy was fingerprinted.

Two days earlier, immediately after the helicopter carried Mary Jo Buttafuoco to Nassau County Medical Center, detectives began a painstaking physical exam of the area surrounding One Adam Road West. They measured the stoop and lifted fingerprints from the wooden railings, the front door, and doorbell. Detectives collected bloodstains for serology tests, storing the samples in a brown paper bag to keep away damaging sunlight. They picked up the live rounds on the stoop and the gun's ejector from the bushes for ballistics testing.

When Amy Fisher's parents learned of their

daughter's arrest, they immediately called Christine Edwards-Neumann, the attorney they had used when Amy was beaten up in school in her sophomore year. Over the years, Edwards-Neumann had also become a family friend. Her home-based office in Freeport was just a short drive from Stitch 'n Sew.

Oddly, Edwards-Neumann had the Fishers on her mind that morning. After the criminal suit against the girl who broke Amy's nose had been settled, she had promised the Fishers she would file a civil suit. Busy with other cases, she'd put it off. But the day before, just about the time Amy was picked up by police, Chris Edwards-Neumann spent a few hours putting together the appropriate papers. In the morning she slipped the papers into a gray linen envelope, then realized she didn't have stamps.

She decided to make a cup of tea. She would then go to the post office to send off the lawsuit. The teakettle whistled just as the phone rang. It was Elliot Fisher, with the terrible news about Amy.

As Edwards-Neumann listened, astonished, she spilled her tea and burned her foot. This couldn't be the little girl she knew.

In the middle of the conversation, the Fishers' call waiting clicked. It was Paul from the gym.

"Have you heard anything about Amy?" he asked.

"Yes," Elliot Fisher snapped. "They picked her up last night. She's being arraigned for the attempted murder of Joe Buttafuoco's wife. That motherfucker. I knew he was boffing my daughter for a long time. That son of a bitch lied to me. I knew that son of a bitch was lying. I can't believe he got my daughter in all this trouble."

"Mr. Fisher, I'm really sorry," Paul said. "If there's anything I can do . . ."

"Thanks, Paul. Look, I'm really upset right now. I'm just sick. I got to go. I've got the lawyer on the other line. I'll talk to you another time."

Elliot Fisher spoke with Edwards-Neumann for only a few minutes. She told him she needed to call police headquarters. At once.

"You stay put," she said. "Don't talk to anybody."

Minutes later Edwards-Neumann got Detective Severin on the line. The attorney quickly asked what they were doing with Amy. He told her—taking a videotaped confession.

"We have a fatal attraction case here," he said.

"Listen, I want you to stop what you're doing," Edwards-Neumann cut in. "I want to see her."

"I don't think that's in her best interest," Severin responded.

"It certainly is in her best interest. I want to see her right away. What has she been charged with?"

"Well, I have a meeting scheduled with Fred Klein this morning. She's being held."

"That wasn't the question. I asked what she's been charged with."

"We don't quite know yet. We're not ultimately responsible for charging her. The DA is."

"If you have to give me a guesstimate . . ."

"Why don't you call back around twelve?"

"I'd like to meet with the client."

"She's still with us. We're not ready for you."

"That may be so," Edwards-Neumann snapped sarcastically. "It might be said that police and detectives are never ready for lawyers. But I'm ready for her. And my guess is she's been ready for me all night long."

The attorney did not see Amy Fisher until 3:00 P.M. that afternoon, when the seventeen-year-old was brought to first district court in Hempstead in handcuffs, set to be arraigned on charges of attempted murder, criminal use of a firearm, two counts of assault, and two counts of criminal possession of a weapon. The maximum sentence for her crimes: 12½ to 25 years in prison.

In nearby Freeport the "closed" placard on the door of Stitch 'n Sew looked strange on this Friday afternoon. Except during the annual vacation they took with their daughter, the Fishers had opened the store every morning promptly at 10:00 A.M., ready for the first customers requesting matching buttons or custom reupholstering.

That day the Fishers did not think of their business. They didn't know it then, but within six weeks they would close Stitch 'n Sew for good, a casualty of the enormous emotional and financial burden they would face. By that time it would hardly matter. Giving up the business they had toiled to build for almost two decades paled in comparison with losing their daughter.

Just before 1:00 P.M. a public information officer from police headquarters called the Nassau

County Courthouse pressroom. Ever since the shooting reporters had checked in with the cops every day, eager for updates. On this afternoon a television reporter took an important call.

"Heads up," the officer said. "Told you something big was about to break on that Buttafuoco case. We've got the shooter—it's a seventeen-year-old girl, having an affair with the lady's husband. We're taking her in at three."

"Holy shit," the reporter said. Holding the phone, she shouted the news to the others. "They've got a teenager in connection with the shooting. Kid was having an affair with the woman's husband. Perp walk at three." (A "perp walk" refers to the area where police bring prisoners by van to the courthouse. It's always in the same place.)

Outside first district court, television cameras and photographers waited for Amy's arrival. In handcuffs, Amy, led by two detectives, turned the corner and for the first time faced the cameramen and photographers who would haunt her for months to come. The moment she saw the cameras, Amy ducked, her hair spilling across her face. That scene of Amy, in her skimpy shorts and T-shirt, on her way to face a judge for the first time, played repeatedly on the evening news, occasionally in slow motion. The announcers intoned the story: "In a case of teenage fatal attraction, little Amy Fisher, the Long Island Lolita, is charged with shooting her lover's wife."

Inside the courtroom, Amy sat in the corner of the detention area, weeping. The high school senior looked completely out of place. Her case was the last to be called for the day. In the near empty courtroom Rose and Elliot Fisher sat together in bewilderment as Chris Edwards-Neumann asked the judge for a few moments to talk to Amy.

They met in the corner of the courtroom, talking in hushed voices. A few minutes later Amy stood motionless before District Court Judge Bruce Alpert. It had been almost twenty-four hours since police had pulled over her car on Merrick Road. Since then she had barely slept and hadn't eaten at all. She listened as Assistant District Attorney Fred Klein cemented her fate.

"Your Honor, we have a very strong case," he said. "We can prove she purchased the gun, was driven to that location, rang the doorbell, and with a twenty-five-caliber automatic handgun shot the victim and left her on the doorstep to die. . . . She then disposed of the gun and clothing that was bloody . . . and attempted an alibi."

Edwards-Neumann tried to minimize Klein's attack. She pointed out that Amy had never been in trouble with the law before and that the girl's parents were local business owners who would watch their daughter.

But Klein was prepared and determined to keep Amy in jail. He reached for a copy of the missing persons report Elliot Fisher had filed the year before. Amy, he told Alpert, was totally uncontrollable. Just ask her family.

Amy's parents didn't move. They sat close, their shoulders touching. Their nightmare was about eighteen hours old.

Judge Alpert ordered Amy held without bail but granted Edwards-Neumann's request for protective custody. Without a backward glance, Amy Fisher was removed to the youth tier of the women's cell block in the Nassau County Correctional Facility in East Meadow. She entered a six-by-eight-foot cell, collapsed on the bed by the wall, and stared at the ceiling. Guards closed the door with a clang.

A little while later Amy asked to use the telephone. She called Paul at the gym, collect.

"Paul, I'm in jail," she said, crying. "I can't believe it. I really screwed up. I'm in trouble."

"Amy, please tell me you're not involved in any of this," Paul said gently. "You couldn't be that fucking stupid."

"I don't know. I don't know. I can't talk about it," Amy said. "Paul, if I have to stay here, I'll kill myself."

"Just hang in there," he said. "It's going to be okay."

The next morning two detectives showed up at Paul's house. The gym owner wasn't surprised.

"I know why you're here," Paul said, pushing open the screen door.

"Why?"

"You're here because of Amy Fisher. You want to know who drove her and who got her the gun. Come on in."

For the next two hours Paul explained his friendship with Amy and what he knew about her relationship with Joey Buttafuoco. Detectives told

123

Paul some of what they'd heard about him from Joey Buttafuoco. Paul shook his head in amazement. Joey had an interesting version of the truth.

When detectives finished questioning Paul they said they believed he wasn't involved in the shooting but needed to do more investigating.

"You'll find whoever was with her," Paul said as they left. "You won't be back here."

He was right. The detectives never returned.

Within a few days, however, the media pounced on Future Physique with verve. Camera crews began showing up daily, wanting to film the gym where Amy and Joey had trained. When reporters asked for him, Paul, with a straight face, often said that he was very sorry but Paul was out of town and couldn't be reached. When cornered, he admitted he was a casual friend of Amy's but didn't elaborate. Some news reports described Amy as having a crush on Paul. They said the young gym owner didn't even know her feelings for him.

Paul kept the truth quiet. He was unhappy about the publicity and worried that all this fuss gave his gym a bad name. And he was tired of the relentless questions about Amy. Some nights he thought of how much trouble Amy had caused— how she'd steadily lied to him and gotten herself in a terrible mess.

But then he remembered the other side. He thought about that first night they met, when Amy looked like a little kid swinging on the gym bars, laughing. So carefree and full of life. He wondered what had happened to her.

Chapter Fourteen

Edwards-Neumann was eager to take Amy's case. She liked the girl and her parents. From the little she'd heard about how detectives interrogated Amy, the attorney suspected there would be a strong argument that the teenager's civil rights had been denied. But Edwards-Neumann knew she was not the right one for this case. She was not an expert in criminal law, and the Fishers needed one.

Edwards-Neumann had been a Long Island attorney for eighteen years, beginning in a family-run business with her father, brother, and brother-in-law. She'd met the Fishers several years earlier, after her basset hound, Chesterfield, energetically chewed her sofa pillows to threads. Ordering new cushions at Stitch 'n Sew, Edwards-Neumann began to chat with Rose. Rose Fisher told her about Amy and the awful fight she'd recently had at school. She told her how another girl had broken Amy's nose and that her child was in tremendous pain.

"I hope you're doing something about that," Edwards-Neumann said. "You don't seem like the kind of people who sue, but hell, the school didn't stop this from happening. You could get some money for your medical bills, and maybe something to put away for your daughter's college education."

With that, Chris Edwards-Neumann was hired to handle the lawsuit against the school district. In a short time she became a family friend.

Shortly after she hung up with Detective Severin the morning she learned of Amy's arrest, Edwards-Neumann called Eric W. Naiburg, a smooth-talking, high-priced Suffolk County attorney. In the last few years Naiburg had won acquittals for his clients in several celebrated murder cases. Many of his clients were young people, and Edwards-Neumann recalled that Naiburg had two young daughters of his own. She knew his reputation—he was considered pompous and showy. It didn't matter. With Naiburg at the helm, Amy Fisher stood a better chance in court. That was all that mattered to the Fishers and to Chris Edwards-Neumann.

When she phoned Naiburg's Hauppage office, Edwards-Neumann's hand was shaking. Naiburg's secretary said the attorney was upstate at his summer home with his family.

"This is about a very important case," Chris Edwards-Neumann said. "If I don't hear from him in the next ten minutes, I'm going to have to call someone else."

The secretary promised to try to reach Naiburg, and Chris Edwards-Neumann hung up, beginning to consider alternatives. She knew this case needed someone with media savvy.

The phone rang. It was Naiburg's partner, Marty Effman. They talked for a few minutes, after which he put her in touch with Eric Naiburg.

"You don't know me," Edwards-Neumann began, "but I know your reputation. I have a little girl here in a tremendous amount of trouble."

She told him what she knew and said she didn't feel qualified to take on the case. Naiburg suggested Elliot and Rose Fisher meet with him upstate the next day.

"Can you handle the arraignment?" Naiburg asked.

Edwards-Neumann said she could. That morning she typed up a notice of appearance. Later that afternoon she did her best before the judge. Amy, however, was held without bail.

Early the next morning Elliot and Rose Fisher drove several hours upstate to meet with Naiburg. The attorney, usually clad in expensive suits, looked different in his summer home in the mountains. He chain-smoked Now cigarettes and listened to the Fishers' story. His most prominent case had been in 1985, when he represented James Troiano, an eighteen-year-old accused of the satanic cult murder of a Long Island teenager. After Naiburg won an acquittal for his client, no case seemed too complex.

Naiburg immediately began to map out a plan for the Fishers. There was a great deal to do. The first step was to get Amy out on bail. He needed unlimited access to her in order to build a strong defense. Ballistics experts had to be hired to testify about the firing of the gun, its position, and the entry of the bullet wound. Naiburg would need to retain investigators to gather proof of Joey Buttafuoco's affair with the Fishers' daughter. If they decided to argue that Amy was emotionally wrecked by the affair and did not have criminal intent to kill Mary Jo Buttafuoco, testimony of psychologists and other mental health experts would be essential.

The Fishers agreed to everything. Anything they could do, they would. They'd sacrifice every cent they had to bring their daughter home.

With Amy's defense lawyer hired, Elliot and Rose felt a slight sense of relief. But there was no escape anywhere from the terrible reality of what had happened. When they returned home that evening, they began to feel the intense spotlight on little Berkley Lane. Reporters staked out their home and business. The couple began parking their car around the corner, cutting through the backyard to elude the press.

Eric Naiburg returned from vacation early the following week. On Tuesday, four days after Amy's arraignment, he met with the Fishers and Chris Edwards-Neumann.

The foursome decided it was important to talk

to the press. The news reports on Amy had been terrible in the past few days. Headlines screamed about the fatal attraction case, about the wild child from Merrick. On the evening news, Amy's classmates—some of whom barely knew her—complained that Amy Fisher had brought down the reputation of John F. Kennedy. She was going to spoil graduation.

Perhaps the Fishers could abate the tide of negative assaults on their daughter.

It was Rose Fisher who agreed to talk to a reporter from *Newsday*. The meeting was held in Naiburg's office. Elliot Fisher stayed home, too upset to discuss Amy.

Breaking down in tears, Rose said the articles about her child were untrue and unfair. "She is a teenager, and she had the normal ups and downs of a teenager," she said. "She was always respectful to us. When we told her to call, she called. If there were rules regarding something, she obeyed them. She is the light of our lives. She is everything to us."

Rose pulled out a picture of her husband, his arm around Amy on a beach in St. Thomas, the lovely trip they had taken just five months earlier. "Does this look like a child out of control?" Rose Fisher asked, her voice tinged with anger. "This is my daughter. She is a beautiful, sensitive, and sweet little girl."

Rose Fisher said she and her husband did not know Mary Jo Buttafuoco but were praying for her recovery. "Our hearts go out to Mrs. Buttafuoco and her children," she said, carefully omitting Joey Buttafuoco's name.

When asked how Amy's arrest had affected their lives, Rose Fisher fought back tears. "Words cannot describe this nightmare," she said quietly. "Our friends and families can't come to our home because we are besieged by reporters. We can't go to their homes because reporters follow us everywhere. We can't let our dog into the backyard because they have opened our gates and moved our garbage cans. We are afraid to go into one of our neighborhood supermarkets or get a prescription at a drugstore because our name, our address, has been plastered everywhere. . . . We have to keep our shades drawn all the time. Last night, a TV crew tailed me so closely in my car that if I had stopped short, they would have hit me. We feel like we've brought a plague over our entire neighborhood. Our lives have been shattered."

In her anguish, Rose Fisher had summed it up neatly. The next day a *Newsday* editor chose her quote from the interview with Amy's mother. It was simple, succinct. "Words cannot describe this nightmare."

A week after Amy's arrest, the case went to the twenty-three-member grand jury sitting in Nassau County Court in Mineola. The jury heard testimony from the school nurse, Rose Fisher, Josh, the classmate who took her for a drive that morning, and Amy's hairdresser friend.

But the most riveting testimony came from Mary Jo Buttafuoco herself. In a heartbreaking videotaped interview with Assistant District Attorney Fred Klein, Mary Jo, from her hospital bed, sluggishly gave chilling details about the young girl with the T-shirt, the girl she identified as Amy Fisher.

The site of Mary Jo, heavily drugged, her head bandaged, and racked by pain gave jurors all they needed. The next day the grand jury brought back a true bill, stating there was indeed enough evidence to go to trial. Amy Fisher was indicted.

It didn't seem possible, but the news on Amy got worse. Shortly after the indictment Naiburg told the Fishers that word of Amy's prostitution was about to break in the media. The Fishers suffered through a weekend of tingling headlines.

But the publicity wasn't foremost on their mind. That weekend the Fishers prayed that Amy would be released on bail. She'd been in jail for more than a week, losing weight and emotionally devastated. Whatever she'd done, whatever her problems, Elliot and Rose Fisher desperately wanted their child home. They would see that Amy received the psychological help she needed.

On Tuesday, June 2, at 9:30 A.M., Amy was brought for a bail hearing to Judge Marvin Goodman's courtroom on the third floor of Nassau County Criminal Court. It wasn't auspicious timing. The night before, "A Current Affair" had broadcast its "Lolita tapes." Portraying Amy Fisher as a frightened high school student in need of her parents' support was not going to be easy.

Outside the courtroom, an hour before the arraignment was scheduled to begin, a crush of reporters and photographers jockeyed for position. The court reporter, Bernard Samowitz, was among the first to push his way through the doors.

"Good morning, sports fans," he said to the press sarcastically.

A long line snaked around the corner, almost reaching the elevator banks. Reporters, courtroom gadflies—mostly retirees who attended all celebrity cases—and law students interested in witnessing Naiburg and Klein at work took their seats. By 9:15 all seventy-five seats were filled. The court officers closed the doors and blocked the entrance.

Pandemonium followed. Several reporters from the New York City dailies arrived just as the doors closed. For the next half hour they would alternately argue and cajole, trying to explain the gravity of getting inside. The officers did not budge. The court did not permit people to stand in the back. If the seats were filled, one explained with feigned sympathy, it was too bad. Even if your editor won't understand.

"You should have gotten here earlier," he added, smirking.

The guards did, of course, step aside as Elliot and Rose Fisher made their way through the crowd, with Chris Edwards-Neumann at their side. Reporters hovering outside the door immediately called out questions, not really expecting answers.

"Did you see 'A Current Affair' last night?" "Do you know whether or not that is your daughter on the tape?"

Rose and Elliot did not reply. They had, in fact, watched the show. Chris Edwards-Neumann had spent the evening with them, providing them with the support they needed. Inside the courtroom, the Fishers took their seats on the left side, next to the attorney. Elliot rubbed his face with his hand. His wife worried about his health. The strain of the last few days had been enormous.

Elliot and Rose had to be strong. It was crucial that they show the court they were united in their support for their child. By their very appearance in the courtroom, they hoped to show the judge that they loved Amy, that they would control her and ensure she returned to court when it was time.

Amy entered the courtroom from a back door, her hands cuffed behind her. She wore dark pants and a black-and-white print shirt. She stood next to Naiburg, in front of the judge. She never once looked at her parents.

Chapter Fifteen

The clerk spoke first.

"Indictment 81927, *People* versus *Amy Fisher*. Step up please. You are Amy Fisher?"

AMY: Yes.

CLERK: You appear here with your attorney, Mr. Naiburg, for arraignment?"

AMY: Yes.

CLERK: Amy Fisher, on May 29, 1992, the Grand Jury of the County of Nassau, State of New York, under indictment 81927, indicted you for the crimes of attempted murder in the second degree; criminal use of a firearm in the first degree, an armed felony; assault, first degree, two counts, one count of which is an armed felony; criminal possession of a weapon in the second degree, an armed felony; and criminal possession of a weapon in the third degree, an armed felony. . . .

How do you plead to the indictment, guilty or not guilty?

AMY: Not guilty.

Those were the only words required of Amy Fisher. Now it was all up to Eric Naiburg.

For the next ten minutes the defense attorney proffered an alternative impression of Amy Fisher: a seventeen-year-old child, frightened and distraught.

Amy, argued Naiburg, had never been in trouble with the law before. Born and raised in Nassau County, Amy Fisher had strong roots in the community. Her entire family—her parents, grandparents, aunts, and uncles—were all Long Island residents. It was all she knew. She didn't have any money, no opportunity to flee. With all the publicity swirling around her case, she couldn't escape unnoticed anyway.

Naiburg pointed to Elliot and Rose Fisher, motionless in the front row. "They will assure this court by word and deed that Amy will return when this court mandates it," he said. "I stand here authorized to say to this court that they are willing to put everything they have, everything they own, on the line. I don't think there's any greater confidence that can be shown to this court of her intentions to return, than the people that have worked their whole lives to save, to buy a home, to make a future for themselves in retirement, than to say that I am willing to risk it all. That's how confident we are that Amy will return to the jurisdiction of this court and abide by the processes of this court."

Naiburg asked the judge to consider Amy's education. She was just a few weeks from graduation. The principal at her school had promised to arrange for a private tutor to work with Amy at home in Merrick, preparing her to take the exams she needed to graduate.

At the end of his argument Naiburg stressed Amy's frail emotional health. He told a hushed courtroom that Amy was devastated by what had happened, that she needed her family and the help of a counselor. Naiburg did not mention Joey Buttafuoco by name, but his allusion to the auto body repairman was plain.

"She is in a crisis situation and has suffered trauma because of the abuse that she has suffered at the hands of another person involved in this case," he said. "Judge, I have to get help for her . . . I have to have her home for that. She needs this kind of attention over the next couple of months . . . a psychologist or psychiatrist who will help her understand the difficulties she is going through, help her to assist me in her defense."

Naiburg paused. He glanced down at his notes, then faced the judge squarely.

"I have represented clients who have been charged with much more serious crimes, murder, and have been released on bail. I am not asking that she be released on her own recognizance, but I am asking that the bail set be reasonable and affordable, to assure her return to court."

"I don't mean to interrupt," Judge Goodman said, "but what do you say is reasonable and affordable?"

"Fifty thousand dollars, Your Honor. I am willing to make fifty thousand dollars bail. . . . All I could add, I guess, is that I personally have no concern about Amy attempting to flee the jurisdiction. It's just not going to happen."

Naiburg sat down. Amy's parents held hands tightly. It was Fred Klein's turn. The prosecutor came out swinging. He reminded the court that bail was not an automatic right of a defendant. And in this case it was a dangerous idea. Quoting Section 510.30 of the Criminal Procedure Law, Klein outlined the criteria for setting bail. It was based on the seriousness of the crime, strength of the case against the defendant, the defendant's likelihood of flight, and, finally, the danger to the community if the defendant should be released.

One by one Klein ticked off reasons why Amy Fisher must remain in jail. Interestingly, while Naiburg had repeatedly referred to Amy as "a seventeen-year-old child," Klein regularly called Amy "this woman" or "the defendant."

"Judge, I suggest to the court that this is about as serious a case as you could get," he began. "The fact that Mrs. Buttafuoco survived the assault is not something that the defendant intended."

Klein reminded the judge that Mary Jo Buttafuoco was completely blameless. She had simply talked with Amy Fisher on her front porch and was subsequently gunned down without warning.

The prosecution, he stated, had an extremely strong case. They had Mary Jo's eyewitness testimony, as well as written and oral statements from Amy admitting to the shooting. Klein disavowed Amy's insistence that the shooting was an accident.

"The defendant went to Mrs. Buttafuoco's home with a loaded semiautomatic, twenty-five-caliber handgun. What kind of accident is this?" he said. "The defendant's conduct after the shooting is completely inconsistent with an accident. She did not call for help. Students, friends, even her own family who saw the defendant within minutes and hours and days of the shooting have confirmed that they saw nothing unusual in the defendant's conduct during this period of time after the shooting—hardly, hardly an indication of a woman who accidentally shot a stranger in the head."

As journalists fervently scratched notes, Klein told the court that Amy Fisher had been planning to kill Mary Jo Buttafuoco for almost nine months, that she'd talked about it to many people and had hired a young man to help her. Once, last fall, Klein said, Amy and the other teen had even gone to the Buttafuoco home in a botched attempt to kill Mary Jo.

The image of a frightened high school student in need of her family was quickly vanishing.

Klein hammered away. He brought up the missing persons report and Amy's prostitution, pointing out the teenager's scheme to cheat the escort service. In his conclusion he left little doubt that Amy Fisher was a reckless, unstable woman with deleterious designs on the Buttafuoco family.

"Your Honor, I suggest to the court that the likelihood of flight of this defendant in this case is astronomical," he said. "One might describe this defendant as a seventeen-year-old girl who lives home with her parents and goes to high school. That would be about as accurate, Your Honor, as describing John Gotti as a businessman from New York City. This is not your typical seventeen-year-old high school student."

Amy, he said, had told police she didn't like her parents, that they had no relationship. It didn't matter how much money her parents put up for her bail. She'd run anyway.

"It would mean nothing to this defendant for her to flee and her parents to lose everything," he said. "Look at what she has already put them through. . . . Your Honor, this defendant is uncontrollable, unstable, manipulative, violent, and extremely dangerous. I respectfully ask you to deny bail at this time. If you must set bail—and I strongly recommend against it—I suggest that it be in an amount of at least two million dollars."

Naiburg attempted to refute some of Klein's charges, but it was too late. Judge Goodman had made up his mind. He granted the prosecution's request, setting Amy Fisher's bail at $2 million, the highest in the history of Nassau County, Long Island.

Legal experts were startled, noting myriad cases of defendants accused of murder who had been released on far lower bail. But those who knew Judge Marvin Goodman were not surprised. Over the years the balding Goodman had earned a reputation as tough on the defense. A judge for almost two decades, he had presided over another celebrity case just two years earlier: the trial of Robert Golub, a twenty-two-year-old bodybuilder convicted of murdering his thirteen-year-old neighbor, Kelly Ann Tinyes. In that case no one could argue with Goodman's stiff sentence for the young man—twenty-five to life. But, the Fisher case appeared far less straightforward. It didn't matter. Whatever dollar figure Fred Klein picked, it was pretty assured that Judge Goodman would agree.

"Goodman is rough," said one attorney who knows him well. "Eric Naiburg didn't get a good draw with him. Whatever the DA says, goes. Goodman just rubber-stamps the DA's office. Like a judge in traffic court—whatever the cop says, goes."

The courtroom emptied quickly. Reporters hurried to the side of the building, eager to catch Amy as she was taken back to jail. Photographers squashed by the front door, anxious to snap a picture of the grieving family. As Amy was led out the back door of the courtroom, she turned to

Naiburg, distraught. She glanced at Fred Klein, gathering his papers on the table.

"How can he stand up there and lie like that?" she asked.

Naiburg pressed his hand to her shoulder. "Unfortunately," he said, "at a bail hearing they can say anything they want without restriction. Now, don't worry. I'm going to appeal this right away. Today. You be strong. Okay?"

Amy nodded, steeling herself. She knew she would face a barrage of journalists in minutes.

With two armed guards on either side, she was taken down by a back elevator to the court's basement and brought out to a waiting sheriff's van. A fusillade of camera shutters began to snap. Questions flew.

"Amy, who was the driver?"

"Amy, was that you on the tape?"

Elliot and Rose left through a different door. Reporters had staked it out as well.

"Can you make the two-million-dollar bail?"

"How are you feeling?"

Naiburg stayed behind to address the media. He stopped a few feet out of the courtroom and began to talk but was shouted down by frustrated reporters who couldn't hear him. The attorney found a corner spot by the stairs around the bend from Judge Goodman's third-floor chambers.

"Mr. Buttafuoco's involvement is much deeper than the DA is letting you know," he said. "Mr. Buttafuoco was the individual that got Amy Fisher involved with ABBA escort service. This man is someone who used and abused her. I have personal knowledge that he is nothing more than what I have alleged. He should be brought to task for this someday. . . . We are not painting Amy as a pure, innocent little girl. She has a tremendous amount of problems. Mr. Buttafuoco is on the top of the list. He's the pimp who put her in the damn business. He *is* the escort service. He abused this young child. He took advantage, he took her innocence."

Eric Naiburg held up his hands. The press conference was finished. He tucked his briefcase under his arm and began heading downstairs.

"Eric," shouted a television news reporter. "Who do you want to play you in the movie?"

Eric Naiburg looked up at the large crowd, television cameras trained on him. His blue eyes sparkled, and he tried to suppress a smile. "I'll tell you, if you turn that thing off," he said, gesturing to the camera.

Back in the courtroom, artists were touching up their work. Bernard Samowitz, the court reporter, peeked at the images as he made his way out of the courtroom. He laughed to himself. The artists's renderings and the scene he'd just witnessed were amazingly different.

"You could hardly see Amy's face, and the artists are drawing her with her hair back," he said later. "She was wearing something where you couldn't tell what kind of figure she had, and the artist gave her a little figure. Her face was very plain, the artist pursed her lips, gave her a sensual feeling. They want to get that violence, mystery, and sex. Always the sex, because it sells.

143

The artists were out to make her sexual and sensual and older than her years. It just wasn't so. She looked like a little kid."

That evening in Merrick, Amy's parents lay in bed in the dark, too upset even to speak. They heard a light tap at the back door, and Elliot Fisher warily made his way downstairs. Rose Fisher stayed upstairs, too distraught to join him.

"It's Sally North," a voice said quietly. "I won't ask any questions."

Elliot opened the door. Not ordinarily a demonstrative man, he hugged his next-door neighbor. They stood in the doorway for a few moments, holding each other tightly.

His voice unsteady, Elliot Fisher broke the silence. "Our lives are shattered," he said almost in a whisper. "I don't know how we're going to go on."

He apologized to Sally North, saying he and his wife were very sorry for the shame brought to the neighborhood. They felt terrible about the media spotlight on little Berkley Lane. Sally North shook her head vehemently, trying to reassure him. No one in the neighborhood felt that way, she told him earnestly. No one was upset with the Fishers. They were angry at the media for sensationalizing the story.

In the doorway, Elliot told Sally about that terrible night Amy didn't come home, how he'd called the police throughout the night, how they'd never told him they were questioning his daughter.

Sally listened, her heart aching. Before she left she gave him a plate of food, leftovers from her daughter's bat mitzvah that weekend. She made him promise that he would call on her if he or Rose needed anything.

As she turned to go, Elliot Fisher stopped her with these chilling words.

"You have three daughters; be careful," he said. "Keep a close eye on them, because somebody can just come one day and turn them completely around."

Sally North nodded, her eyes filled with tears. She walked through the backyard to her door. She has played those words over in her head many times since.

Chapter Sixteen

$\mathbf{F}$ollowing the bail hearing, a disturbing picture of Amy's prolonged intent to kill Mary Jo Buttafuoco began to emerge in pieces. Two young men stepped into the media blitz to share their stories.

One was Christopher Drellos, the nineteen-year-old former classmate of Amy's from Kennedy High School whom she dated briefly the spring before her affair with Joey. Chris had been a senior at Kennedy when Amy was a sophomore. Although he had transferred and eventually graduated from Calhoun High School in 1990, he and Amy had remained friends.

In the winter of 1991, around the time Amy left home and stayed with her grandmother for two weeks, Chris told Amy he was planning to leave his parents' Levittown house and rent a place of his own. Amy was impressed. She told him she hoped to do the same. She said she was unhappy at home—her parents didn't understand her and treated her like a child. Recently they had tried to enforce a new edict—that she drive the Dodge only to and from school or work. Amy managed to slip around their rules as she had in the past, but her parents were hassling her and she'd had enough. Chris and Amy discussed the possibility that Amy would rent a room in his new place. Amy gave him money as a down payment.

Amid this turbulent time in Amy's life, she and Chris began to date. Chris made it clear he wasn't interested in a committed relationship. They never went to lunch or to the movies—they usually just met somewhere for sex. For Chris Drellos it was an ideal setup. No responsibilities, no hassles. For Amy it was the start of a new pattern of using sex to feel loved.

The relationship was so casual that it didn't surprise Chris Drellos to learn later that in early July Amy had begun to see someone else. That her new lover was a married man in his mid-thirties, however, was a bit of a jolt.

Chris first learned about Amy's affair with Joey Buttafuoco in August. He had mentioned that he wanted pinstripes for his car—something like the bright pink stripes on Amy's Dodge. Amy immediately suggested Complete Auto Body. That's where her customizing had been done, she told him. And she had a good friend there—the guy who ran the place.

When Chris and Amy pulled into the garage at Complete Auto Body, a mechanic greeted Amy with a wave. She entered the office through a back door, and Joey stepped out from behind his desk.

Amy introduced him to Chris Drellos. The young man explained what he wanted, and Joey promptly called a mechanic to get started.

Joey motioned to Amy.

"I'll be back," the young girl said to Chris, following Joey upstairs.

For forty-five minutes Drellos paced the garage, puzzled. What was Amy up to? What was the deal with this guy? Chris couldn't help but notice the pictures of Joey's wife and kids hanging on the wall. What the hell was going on?

By the time Amy reappeared, flustered and a bit giggly, Drellos could barely contain his curiosity. He settled the bill, and waited until he and Amy were in the car, pulling out of the repair shop. He turned to look at Amy.

"What's going on with you two?" he asked. "What were you guys doing up there?"

"He's my boyfriend," Amy responded lightly. "Great sex."

"You're kidding. Isn't he married?"

"Yeah. Two kids. It's okay. His wife doesn't know anything. Joey's careful."

There was silence.

"He's madly in love with me," Amy said suddenly. "Joey really loves me a lot."

Chris shrugged. He pulled into the driveway on Berkley Lane. There didn't seem to be much to say. News of Amy's affair with the auto repairman surprised him. He thought it strange that Amy seemed so taken by that guy. Thirty-five seemed awfully old.

But Amy's dalliance with Joe Buttafuoco didn't

bother Chris Drellos at all. Frankly, he didn't care who Amy slept with. For the last few months his association with Amy Fisher had been optimal: uncomplicated sex and no demands. Amy never asked him for anything.

A few days after the pinstriping, however, she did.

One August afternoon Amy asked Chris Drellos to get her a gun. Amy explained her reason matter-of-factly: the only way she could have Joey to herself was to get rid of his wife. Chris turned out to be the first person Amy ever spoke to about killing Mary Jo Buttafuoco.

Chris listened halfheartedly. He didn't believe Amy would ever shoot this woman. He tried to change the subject, but Amy was persistent. "I need a gun," she told him. "I'm serious. I'd do anything to see Mrs. Buttafuoco die because I want Joey. He's the only one I love."

Amy reminded Chris that he still owed her the rent money she'd given him months before. He began to get annoyed. His carefree fling with the pretty high school classmate was getting to be more trouble than it was worth.

Chris put Amy off for a few days. "Let me think about it," he told her.

Amy continued to call him.

"If you're not going to get me a gun," Amy snapped one day, "then you'd better give me my money back."

Exasperated, Chris Drellos devised a solution: he would introduce Amy to Stephen Sleeman, a twenty-one-year-old neighbor who had been a good friend of Chris's older brother for six years. Sleeman had a gun—a .22-caliber rifle he used for target practice. Chris knew the five-foot-two, stocky Vietnamese man would never shoot anyone. But Amy didn't know that.

Chris was almost giddy. Amy would surely end up having sex with Sleeman. Chris would get her off his back and provide his buddy with a pretty girl. She'd even pay the guy. Perfect.

Chris didn't know what to make of Amy Fisher. By this time Amy had told him about her married man and working for the escort service. Chris had even given Amy rides to meet a few clients.

Amy wasn't like any girl he'd ever known. He thought she was a bit loony, with this crazy escort service and all. And now all this talk about a murder. It was definitely time to dump this girl.

When Chris called Stephen Sleeman in mid-August, he kept the story brief. There was this girl, Amy, he said, a girl he ought to meet. "Go along with her," he said with a laugh. "She'll give you all the sex you want."

Just days before Amy's seventeenth birthday, Chris took her to Michael's, a family-style seafood eatery on the Nautical Mile in Freeport, where Stephen Sleeman had recently begun working as a waiter. Sleeman stopped by their table briefly— it was a busy evening and he couldn't really talk. He checked out the attractive girl in shorts and a sleeveless T-shirt. He and Amy exchanged beeper numbers, and Chris gave him a knowing smile.

A few days later Amy punched in Sleeman's

beeper number. He was home, watching television. He called her back right away.

Amy didn't waste time. She told him about her married boyfriend, and about her boyfriend's wife. She said she'd heard Sleeman had a rifle. Maybe they could make a deal.

"I love Joey," she explained. "He's the only one I love. I have to be with him."

There was a pause. "Will you shoot Mrs. Buttafuoco for me?" she asked.

On the other end of the phone, Stephen Sleeman listened in amazement. He put his feet up on the table and tried not to laugh.

"Sure," he told her. "I'll do it."

Stephen Sleeman had his own agenda. A soft-spoken young man with a nervous laugh, he didn't have much experience with girls. Here was a tantalizing invitation indeed. A dark-haired beauty offering money and sex. "I was looking to get laid," Sleeman explained later. "I never really thought she was serious."

Sleeman grew up in Levittown, just a few miles from Amy. He'd been adopted by Sally and Joe Sleeman when he was one year old. Sally, a nurse, and Joe, a *Daily News* circulation employee, were loving parents but had recently separated. Joe Sleeman had moved out.

Sleeman wasn't exactly a stellar student at St. Dominik's, the Catholic high school in Oyster Bay he'd graduated from a year earlier. But the young man was hardworking and had a clear vision of his future. One day he hoped to open his own restaurant. To that end he attended business classes at the local community college and took the job at Michael's, advancing from busboy to waiter to chef in just a few months.

In the two months that followed that first August phone conversation with Amy Fisher, Sleeman landed another job: stalking Mary Jo Buttafuoco.

For Sleeman it was more a prank than a plot to murder. Almost every day, in between classes and before his shift at the restaurant, Sleeman drove to Massapequa and parked his white Plymouth Horizon in the marina next to One Adam Road West. Amy expected a full report—what time Mary Jo went shopping, when she returned, if anyone visited, and for how long.

Sleeman wasn't exactly diligent about his detective work. Most days he showed up to his post late, gazed at the bay for a few minutes, and promptly fell asleep. When Amy pulled up in her LeBaron a short time later, she'd tap on the window, annoyed, and wake him.

"I just fell asleep this second," Sleeman would confess, chagrined.

Amy kept her part of the bargain. She paid Sleeman a lump sum of $400 and in the next few months turned over $200 more in tens and twenties. In Sleeman's car by the marina, Amy also gave him oral sex. When Sleeman's story broke in the New York City tabloids, the *Daily News* headline was PAID ME IN SEX. The *Post* got more graphic: AMY'S HORNY HITMAN. *New York Newsday* just groaned, OH AMY, OH AMY, OH AMY.

Their first sexual contact occurred in Amy's

153

LeBaron. Sleeman was driving on the freeway when Amy suddenly leaned over and unzipped his pants.

"What are you doing?" the young man asked, stunned.

"Just relax."

Amy gave him oral sex. When they were done she zipped his pants calmly.

"There," she said, laughing. "I couldn't let you get out with your pants unzipped."

Amy's flagrant promiscuity astonished Stephen Sleeman. A short time after they met, Amy told him she carried a beeper for her job. "I work for an escort service," she told him. "Men beep me, and I go with them. It's also for Joey. He beeps me and we go out."

Sleeman wasn't sure whether to believe her. When she gave him the $400, he asked more questions.

"Where are you getting all this money from?"

"I already told you," Amy said. "I sleep with men for money."

A few times she asked him to drive her to ABBA, where she'd drop off vouchers and pick up cash.

Sometimes she'd talk about her clients. She said she didn't allow any of them to kiss her, and proudly maintained that she always remained in control. Once, Sleeman asked her about condoms.

"Do you bag those guys?" he asked.

"Everyone except Joey," she said. "It's different with Joey. I fuck those guys. Joey and I make love."

It was an important distinction for Amy. After

On Wednesday, May 20, 1992, Amy Fisher, a 17-year-old high school senior, was arrested for the attempted murder of Massapequa resident Mary Jo Buttafuoco.

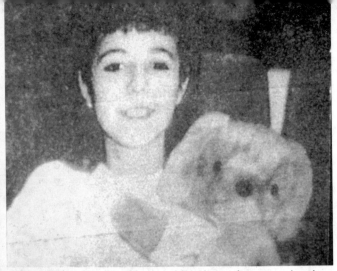

Amy Fisher had a privileged middle-class upbringing. Amy's parents satisfied her every whim, including giving her an expensive car. She also had her own personal beeper. (*"A Current Affair"*)

The Fisher house on Berkley Lane in Merrick, Long Island. Amy's car is shown parked in the driveway. (*Dean Surh*)

Joey Buttafuoco claims that his relationship with Amy Fisher was purely platonic. "Mary Jo's my high school sweetheart... I've been dying to be with a 37-year-old woman all my life...." (*Mary McLoughlin*, © New York Post)

Complete Auto Body is the Buttafuoco family business where Joey was employed. Amy and her father brought her wrecked 1989 Dodge Daytona in for repairs before Christmas 1990. The affair Amy says she had with Joey began six months later. *(Dean Surh)*

Joey's boat *Double Trouble*, docked in the marina near his home, was the site of the affair Amy claimed they had, which she said began just before her 17th birthday on July 2, 1991. *(Dean Surh)*

The stoop of Joey and Mary Jo Buttafuoco's waterfront Massapequa home. At 11 A.M. on Tuesday, May 19, Amy Fisher allegedly arrived here, spoke briefly with Mary Jo, and then pulled out a loaded .25-caliber Titan semiautomatic pistol and shot her.
(Dean Surh)

The Baldwin, New York residence of ABBA, an escort service where Amy was employed.
(Dean Surh)

Mary Jo, shown being escorted by Joey after the incident, believes her husband's story: "I love my Joey. My Joey loves me." (© 1992 *Dick Yarwood*, Newsday)

Mary Jo, shown here with her son, Paul, after the shooting, has been permanently injured. She is paralyzed on the right side of her face, deaf in her right ear and has double vision in her right eye.
(*Mary McLoughlin*, © New York Post)

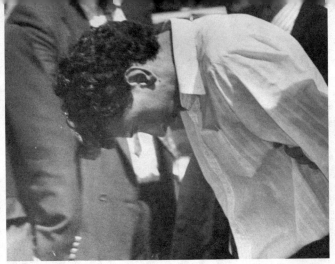

Peter Guagenti, a Brooklyn auto-parts store worker, allegedly sold Amy the gun she used to shoot Mary Jo Buttafuoco. (© 1992 *Dick Kraus*, Newsday)

Rose and Elliot Fisher, shown here coming out of the courthouse, have supported their daughter throughout the crisis. They used up their entire savings to have Amy released on bail, and have sold their upholstery business to pay lawyer fees. (*Mary McLoughlin*, © New York Post)

Amy is greeted by her mother upon arriving home after being released from jail. (© 1992 *Bill Davis*, Newsday)

her arrest, she told Paul, "Joey used to say, 'I don't care who you fuck as long as you love me.'"

Joey's love meant everything to Amy. She talked continuously about how much the repairman cared for her. "Joey loves me," she'd say. "You can't believe how much he loves me."

Sleeman was unimpressed. "If you and this guy are so lovey-dovey, why doesn't he leave his wife?" he once asked.

"Joey loves his wife, and he could never hurt her," Amy replied. "But he could get used to the idea of her not being around."

"Okay." Sleeman shrugged. "But if you have Joe, why do you need so many other people?"

Amy brushed him off, laughing. "I'm bored," she said lightly. "I get bored easily. I like sex. You can't always have it when you want it, so you have to look somewhere else."

That was the image of herself that Amy preferred. Wild and untamed. Always seeking adventure and danger. An escort. A passionate, desirable coquette. The Other Woman. On the outside, Amy was cheerful. She laughed and shocked her friends with her flip comments about sex. Inside, however, her world was crumbling. Desperate for love, she used sex to fill an aching void. Mary Jo Buttafuoco, pretty, married, a mother—as long as she was around, she was living proof of what Amy really wanted.

Twice Sleeman drove her to meet Joey at the Gateway Motel in Merrick. They went out a few times—once bowling with another couple and twice for dinner. Once, dining out with another couple, Amy suddenly asked, "Did you ever fuck anybody on a pool table?" and broke into giggles.

She and Sleeman usually met in their cars by the marina, at Sleeman's house or at Amy's. Sometimes Amy talked about school.

"I'm failing home ec," she'd say almost proudly.

"How can you fail home ec?"

"I don't want to learn how to cook. I have no need for it. I'm failing gym, too. I can't be bothered to run around the track. Why should I get all sweaty?"

Mostly, however, her relationship with Sleeman revolved around a single theme: killing Mary Jo Buttafuoco.

Whenever she talked about the shooting, Sleeman put her off. When she suggested he saw off the handle of his rifle, making it easier to hide under his coat, he did—but took more than a month to do it. Sleeman got adept at coming up with excuses.

But by the end of October Amy had had enough of his stalling. He'd had plenty of time to plan the murder. It was time to put it into action.

On November 1, the day after Halloween, she banged on his front door.

Half-asleep, Sleeman stumbled to answer it.

"I'm tired of your bullshit," Amy said, pushing her way past him. "Grab your rifle. We're doing it today."

He followed her into his bedroom. She plunked down on the edge of his bed, and he began to dress slowly.

"I can't today," he said suddenly. "I have class."

"No, you don't," Amy shot back. "I know your schedule. You don't have school today."

Pulling on his jeans, Sleeman tried again. "I have to work," he said.

"You're off today."

Sleeman tied his sneaker laces, folding the bows slowly.

"We probably can't even get down the block," he said. "There was so much rain yesterday it's probably flooded."

Amy stood up. "I've already been there. It's not flooded. Let's go."

She reached for his rifle behind the door and handed it to him. He slipped it under his coat, unloaded. Surely this girl was crazy if she thought he would actually shoot someone. But he played along.

Amy told him to follow her in his car, and she left her LeBaron on in a restaurant parking lot. She didn't want to bring it to the Buttafuocos.

Once she got into his car, she began to outline the plan. She would ring the doorbell and say she was a student from Massapequa High School selling candy for charity. When Mrs. Buttafuoco stepped outside to buy the candy, Sleeman, hiding at the side of the house, would step forward and shoot. It couldn't be simpler.

When Sleeman pulled over next to One Adam Road West Amy went through the drill one more time. She finished and looked at him, poised, bars of chocolate on her lap.

"You get it?"

Sleeman's thoughts raced. Was she really serious? Did she really expect him to shoot this woman? He slipped the clip-action gun under his long coat and took his position on the north side of the Buttafuoco home, still not certain if this was all a joke. He watched in awe as Amy confidently strolled up the driveway, candy in hand, and rang the front doorbell.

Seconds later Sleeman heard Mary Jo Buttafuoco's voice.

"Can I help you?"

"I'm a student from Massapequa High School," Amy said, "and we're selling this candy as a fundraiser for charity."

Mary Jo stepped out on the stoop. Amy glanced behind her at Sleeman.

"I don't know, honey," Mary Jo said. "The kids have plenty of candy left from Halloween."

"But this is really important," Amy persisted. "I have this quota to sell. All the kids do. Besides, it's for a really good cause. It's for charity. It's really important you buy this candy."

Mary Jo hesitated, then smiled in defeat.

"Okay," she said. "Let me get my purse."

Mary Jo stepped back in the house, and the screen door closed quietly.

Amy whirled around and motioned frantically to Sleeman. It was too late. The young man was already running as fast as he could around the corner to his car. From a safe distance he watched in astonishment as Mrs. Buttafuoco handed Amy money and took the box of candy. He quickly got into the Horizon and bent his head against the steering wheel, his heart pounding.

Amy barely approached the car when she started screaming. "Why didn't you shoot? What's the matter with you? You coward. You're yellow. You chicken-shit! Why didn't you shoot?"

Sleeman started the engine, put the car in drive, and sped up Bayview Avenue. "Amy," he snapped, glancing at her in disgust, "what are you, nuts or something? The gun isn't even loaded."

"What are you talking about?" Amy demanded. "How could you come here without a loaded gun? I want my money back. Every penny. I can't believe you. You're a coward. And you better not go to the police, because if you do, you're in big trouble anyway. I'm going to get this done whether you help me or not."

Sleeman drove her back to her car in silence. Amy continued to rail, demanding a refund. She got out of the car and slammed the door. Sleeman headed home. He propped the rifle behind his bedroom door and breathed a sigh of relief.

Meanwhile Mary Jo Buttafuoco was steaming. Moments after she bought the candy, she noticed the bars had prices stamped on the back. Candy for charity indeed.

"Sonavabitch," she muttered. "She was just trying to make money off me."

Amy didn't call Stephen Sleeman for more than a week. When she finally did, she was calm.

"Okay," she said. "You're not going to do it. Fine. I want a refund, or else give me your gun or get me a gun."

159

Sleeman thought for a minute. He certainly had no intention of giving back the money, long since spent. "I'll give you my gun," he said.

But over the next few months Stephen Sleeman perfected the art of procrastination. He came up with every excuse he could think of.

Several times that winter Amy called Stephen's mother, Sally. "He owes me money," she complained.

"I'm sorry, honey," she responded gently. "I'll certainly get on his case. Paying your bills is important. I'll talk to him about it."

By April Amy was livid. She called Sleeman and exploded.

"You can go fuck yourself," she said. "I found someone to help me. I want a refund or I'm going to get some people I know to beat you up."

"Okay, okay," Sleeman said wearily. "Do it yourself, then. I'll pay you back later."

Amy called a few more times over the next few weeks, complaining about her refund. The last time Sleeman heard from her was Saturday, May 16, just three days before the shooting.

"You still owe me money," Amy said.

"I'll pay you back, I already told you," Sleeman said. "I have to go to work." He cradled the receiver.

Less than a week later, as he broiled the evening's special, a waitress asked him if he heard what happened in Massapequa.

"What?"

"Some lady got shot."

Too bad, Sleeman thought.

Later that night a friend stopped into the restaurant and headed to the back to say hello to Stephen.

"Hey, Steve," he said, poking his head into the kitchen. "Did you hear Amy shot Mrs. Buttafuoco?"

Chapter
Seventeen

For a few days Stephen Sleeman kept quiet. He didn't know what to do. He thought about just showing up at police headquarters, explaining all he knew. He wasn't sure what might happen then.

Every morning he bought the local newspapers and read about Amy. He turned on the television in the evening and watched the scene of Amy being led to her arraignment in handcuffs, hair covering her face. Even after months of listening to Amy's relentless tirade about killing Mary Jo Buttafuoco, Stephen Sleeman was still amazed. He had never expected her actually to go through with it.

His mother, Sally, was just as shocked. She had been talking about Amy that very weekend, telling her older son, Douglas, how vulnerable Amy seemed, how troubled. Douglas, twenty-two, interrupted her, pushing a copy of *Newsday* across the kitchen table.

"Ma, Amy's the girl in the paper," he said. "She's the one that shot that lady in Massapequa."

Sally was speechless. She'd always felt sorry for Amy. She recalled all the phone calls, with Amy wanting money back from Stephen. Sally Sleeman never quite understood what the money was for or why Stephen had not returned it. Reading the paper, she felt tears welling in her eyes. She knew this was a girl who somehow had gotten very mixed up.

That weekend Stephen finally called his dad for advice, giving him an abridged version of what had been going on for the last nine months.

"Maybe I should just go to the police," he said.

"Steve," his father cut in, "you can't just walk into the police and say you agreed to shoot this woman. You have to go in there with a lawyer. Let me make a phone call."

Joe Sleeman called Bruce Parnell, an attorney from Lake Ronkonkoma in Suffolk County he'd once hired to close a real estate deal. Parnell had just left for Florida. His secretary jotted down the information from Sleeman and called the attorney in Naples.

"Joe Sleeman called," she told him. "His son knows something about this Amy Fisher case."

"What's an Amy Fisher?" Parnell asked, confused.

"Oh, some girl shot some lady."

"Is she dead?"

"No."

"Well, does it sound like something really important?"

"Nah. I think it can wait."

"Okay. Tell them I'll be back next week."

Amazingly, as headlines broke daily, Parnell tanned on the beach, blissfully unaware of the case that awaited him at home. When he returned to New York late Wednesday, he set up an appointment to meet the Sleemans on Friday afternoon. He was unprepared for the story Stephen Sleeman unfolded that day in his office.

Before the young man had finished, Parnell reached for the phone. "We have to call the DA's office," he told them. "Right away."

He glanced at his watch. It was a few minutes past 5:00 P.M. He dialed anyway.

"I'm sorry," said a woman who answered the phone. "You'll have to call back Monday."

"You don't understand," Parnell said, irritated. "I have information on an attempted murder case."

"I'm sorry," the woman repeated. "The office of the district attorney closes at four forty-five. Call Monday."

Amazingly, Stephen Sleeman's testimony, a crucial link revealing Amy Fisher's prolonged plan to kill Mary Jo Buttafuoco, had to wait. County offices were closed.

Over the weekend Parnell began to worry about his client. He figured the district attorney's office probably had heard about Stephen Sleeman already. He didn't know what, if anything, they knew. The more Parnell mulled it over, the more anxious he became. What if he walked in with Sleeman and they arrested the kid?

On Sunday he called Stephen's father.

"We have to be careful," Parnell told him. "We don't know what the DA knows. They might send out this big press release—'We have just apprehended Stephen Sleeman, who's involved in a conspiracy to commit murder'—and make this poor kid look terrible. And there's Eric Naiburg. My guess is at the moment Amy Fisher has not mentioned this to Naiburg because he probably would have done something to neutralize this kid right away. He'd come up with a story. If Eric finds out about Stephen coming forward before he comes forward, Eric's going to come out in the press and discredit you. You have to be concerned about what the DA might do, and what Naiburg might do."

Stephen's father sighed. "So what do we do?" he asked.

"I think it's in our best interest to play two ends against the middle," Parnell replied. "Let's consider going to the media with this. This way, no matter what happens, you'll have an opportunity to give your side of the story to the press before someone else does."

"If that's what you think is best," said Joe Sleeman. He couldn't believe his son had gotten into such a mess.

Early Monday morning Bruce Parnell phoned the district attorney's office. Fred Klein took his call.

"My client has some information about the Amy Fisher case," Parnell explained. "He's more than willing to cooperate, only I need to have some guarantees before you talk to him."

Klein was equally evasive. "We're not in the position to grant immunity," he responded. "We need to check out his story. We'll meet you in your office at five P.M."

Parnell hung up the phone, uneasy. He decided he'd better get Stephen to the media quick and make sure his story came out in the right way. He was trying to decide whether to call *Newsday* or Channel 12, the local Long Island television network, when his secretary buzzed him on an intercom.

"Someone from 'A Current Affair' is on the line," she said.

Parnell picked up the phone, astonished how the story had traveled.

"I'm calling from 'A Current Affair,' " the voice barked. "Do you represent Stephen Sleeman, and if so, what, if anything, does he know about Amy Fisher?"

Parnell almost laughed. This case was unbelievable.

"Look, he does know Amy Fisher," he said. "I've got the DA coming down here later today. I'm not sure how we should do this."

"We'll send someone there immediately," the show's rep said.

"Let me call you back."

Parnell called Joe Sleeman. "I think we'd better take out an insurance policy against Stephen being placed in a bad light," he told him. "Let's have this 'Current Affair' guy come in right after we meet with the DA. That way, no matter what the DA decides to do afterward we already have it recorded with the show that Stephen came forward first."

At 5:00 P.M. Fred Klein and the chief of the major offenses bureau showed up to hear Stephen's story. They walked gingerly into Parnell's office. A few days earlier a storm had flooded the main floor. The wood floors and furniture were still damp, and the entire office smelled musty. The two men in suits found a dry seat and faced Stephen Sleeman.

The young man explained what he knew. The two men asked questions and took notes.

Parnell sat back and listened, uncomfortable. He checked his watch. The last thing he needed was the "Current Affair" camera crew to show up early.

They didn't. An hour after Klein and the chief left, the show's van pulled into the law office parking lot. Stephen Sleeman was nervous.

"Let's go ahead with this," Parnell advised. "That way, in the event they do decide to arrest you, at least you will have come forward first and given the public your perception of what your involvement was, rather than these guys coming out making it look like they made this big arrest here. Or Naiburg. He might say, 'Oh, yeah, Amy told us there were these kids trying to use her.' Who the hell knows what he might say?"

Sleeman agreed, taking a deep breath. The film crew set up lights and cameras. Steve Dunleavy went over the agreement with Parnell. He was willing to omit Sleeman's name and not show his face, but he had a condition.

"If his name or face is not known by the broadcast Tuesday, I won't use it," he said. "But if everyone in America knows who he is anyway by that time, I will. We don't want to look ridiculous."

Parnell nodded. It seemed fair.

The cameras rolled, and Dunleavy began to ask questions. Like Peter De Rosa before him, Stephen Sleeman spoke from the shadows. At the end, the young man said how sorry he was about all that had happened.

"If I really knew Amy was serious about this, I would have warned Mrs. Buttafuoco what was about to happen," he said. "I'm sorry this happened to her. My heart goes out to her."

The next day Parnell took Stephen to meet again with Klein, this time in the Nassau County Courthouse. The assistant district attorney said he wanted detectives to debrief the young man.

"Wait a minute," Parnell said. "I let him speak to you so you knew what he had to say. But if you want him to sit down and speak to a police officer, who is not an officer of the court, it's going to be with immunity. In writing."

Klein was cornered. He arranged for immunity. Parnell and Stephen waited until the letter was finished.

When detectives finished their inquiry a few hours later, Stephen promised to turn in his rifle. Parnell then told his client to wait for him in the hallway. The attorney suspected he was going to catch hell from the district attorney's office.

"I've got one other thing to tell you," Parnell said, abashed. "We did this show with 'A Current Affair.' It's going to be broadcast in two and a half hours. Sorry, but I didn't know what you were going to do. I had no basis to trust you. I could have brought this kid in today and you could have locked him up and the kid looks like an idiot, and I would look like an idiot, and I couldn't chance that. He didn't say anything that will jeopardize the prosecution's case. He only told them a very limited version of what he told you."

Surprisingly, Klein didn't seem upset. He told Parnell that detectives had planned to pick up Stephen for questioning anyway, the same day, in fact, that Parnell arranged for him to come forward. Stephen's phone number had appeared repeatedly on Amy's records. Parnell was relieved. So far things had worked out smoothly.

That evening Stephen Sleeman went to the Bellmore home of his best friend, a girl he knew from St. Dominik's and had dated casually, to watch "A Current Affair." The girl did not know about Stephen's relationship with Amy Fisher.

Sitting in her living room with the girl's family, Stephen tried to prepare them.

"Look," he said cautiously, "I'm not going to look like a good guy. I'm just warning you."

The girl and her family laughed. "What's going on?" they kept asking. "What did you do?"

Strains of the opening melody of "A Current

Affair" began. For the next few minutes the family watched in silence. From the darkness on the television screen they heard a familiar voice: that of Stephen Sleeman.

The quiet was broken by Stephen's girlfriend. Glaring at him, she began to cry and ran out of the room. Stephen remained frozen on his chair.

"God, Steve, what did you do?" the girl's mother asked. "I can't believe this."

Stephen followed the girl outside. For the next half hour the two yelled at each other, amid tears.

"How could you lie to me this way?" she sobbed. "How could you betray me?"

"Let me explain," Stephen interrupted. "Just give me a chance. . . ."

"I don't want to hear it. I don't want to hear anything."

"I'm really sorry I hurt you."

His friend couldn't be consoled. An hour later Stephen gave up and went home. He called Parnell at home, crying. When he hung up, exhausted, he dropped off to sleep.

At 9:00 the next morning, Stephen Sleeman bolted out of bed. A reporter from "Hard Copy" was banging on the side door. Shaken, the young man called Chris Drellos, who lived nearby. Chris picked him up, and the two drove to Parnell's Lake Ronkonkoma office.

When they pulled into the parking lot, dozens of reporters pounced. Chris and Stephen ran into the office, jackets over their heads.

Parnell's secretary peered out the window and

saw a group of reporters going through Chris Drellos's car. Chris had left the window open and the door unlocked.

"Christ," said Parnell. "Did you leave anything in there with your name on it?"

"Yeah," answered Chris. "Books and stuff. Papers from school. It's okay. Listen, I want to go on 'A Current Affair.' Can you call those guys?"

The phones rang continuously. Reporters rapped on the door. This was getting interesting. Stephen settled back on a chair and opened a can of diet cola. It exploded all over Parnell's desk.

"Slob," Parnell said with a rueful laugh. "I can't even kick you out of here, with all the reporters outside. It's a zoo in here. This office is like Little Big Horn."

Chris Drellos was persistent. He really wanted to go on "A Current Affair." After all, he said, he knew a lot about Amy Fisher, too.

Parnell tried to question the young man. Did he have a lawyer? What did his parents think of all this?

Chris said he didn't have a lawyer, and what his parents thought was irrelevant. He no longer lived at home.

A few days later Parnell took a cranky phone call from Chris Drellos's lawyer, recently hired by the young man's parents. The Manhattan attorney, Barry Agulnick, accused Parnell of making it seem as though he represented Chris. The two attorneys traded barbs and hung up, aggravated.

Agulnick promptly ordered his client never to

speak to reporters without his consent and quickly nixed any television appearances.

Chris, disappointed, never made it on "A Current Affair." He did, however, get his picture in *Newsday*—sort of. The day after the visit to Parnell's office he and Stephen Sleeman were pictured on the front page, side by side—with jackets over their heads.

Chapter
Eighteen

Tension was high at the Nassau County District Attorney's Office. Every morning local newspapers headlined a fresh leak from the Amy Fisher case. Excerpts of Amy's ten-page written statement to police had recently landed in the news, beneath incendiary headlines. LONG ISLAND LOLITA: JOEY GAVE ME THE GUN, hooted the *Daily News*. AMY: SHE TRIED TO PIN SHOOTING ON LOVER, clucked *Newsday*.

Nassau County District Attorney Denis Dillon was annoyed. He pulled his car into a reserved parking space and bounded up the steps of the courthouse on Old Country Road in Mineola. Concrete statues of eagles guarded each side; a flagpole surrounded by greenery stood in the center. Dillon skipped the elevator, heading for the staircase.

Where were these leaks coming from? Was his staff talking? He strode into his second-floor office, past the cracked windowpane on the brown door that had "District Attorney" stenciled on it in gold lettering. Someone was watching the morning news in the waiting room, stretched back on a mustard-colored chair. On the wall hung Dillon's credo: "It is our goal to prevent the victim of the crime from becoming the victim of the system."

Dillon called a meeting. The Amy Fisher case was rapidly spinning out of control. Fred Klein and Ed Grilli, the department's press representative, maintained they had remained tight-lipped about the case. Days earlier Klein had turned down a request to appear on "Good Morning America" and nixed a lunch date with producers from Columbia Pictures who were eager to negotiate a movie deal.

Grilli, too, had tried to keep a low profile, despite fielding hundreds of calls from the media. Many times Grilli's response was exasperatingly noncommittal: he politely told callers that it was much too early in the case to give any more information. He offered a copy of the indictment against Amy. That was the best he could do.

For the district attorney's office, the Amy Fisher case was clearly like none that had come before. The teenager's attorney kept the pressure on. Before myriad television cameras, Eric Naiburg relentlessly demanded that DA Dillon charge Joey Buttafuoco with statutory rape. After weeks of shrieking headlines about "the wild child," it seemed that sympathy for the teenager had grown. The press kept hounding Dillon and Assistant District Attorney Klein. Why weren't they charging Joey Buttafuoco? What were they waiting for?

A few blocks away at police headquarters, Detective Sergeant Daniel Severin was just as aggravated. Leaks were hindering his investigation as well. He called his own meeting in room 2, Nassau County Police Homicide Division, on the second floor of headquarters. It was a messy, comfortable place, with small bands of cops sipping coffee and discussing strategies, leaning against metal desks.

Severin reminded all twenty-one of homicide's detectives to refrain from comment. The press had reported too much already.

Keeping cops from gossiping wasn't easy. At headquarters the telephone lines had lit up incessantly ever since Amy Fisher had been arrested. "Anything new with the case?" reporters wanted to know. "How about something off the record?"

Many of the detectives had friends among the Long Island cop reporters and occasionally slipped them tips. But this story was different.

One detective, defying his superior's command not to talk to the media, said glumly that the case had spun out of control. "Do you know how many friendships have been destroyed over this?" he said bitterly. "Between the cops, the reporters, the DA's office, people calling all the time, yelling, getting mad. 'You told him this, tell me about that.' They call every day. One hundred calls a day. 'Can you tell me anything off the record? Why don't you arrest Buttafuoco?' Everybody's

177

calling in their sources. Everybody wants to get something no one else has. It's been a nightmare."

The detective said the pressure to press charges against Joey Buttafuoco was immense. "That guy is the biggest asshole, but do you know what would happen if we arrested every guy who was screwing around with a seventeen-year-old girl?" he said. "If we did that every time, we'd be in trouble. Besides, was she sixteen? Was she seventeen? They said it started in the summer. As far as I know they didn't punch a time clock. Everyone keeps saying 'Why don't you arrest him?' For what? For making love with a seventeen-year-old girl? The real story is Mary Jo Buttafuoco got shot."

That, he added, was the bottom line. "The story is Mary Jo Buttafuoco got shot in the head," he repeated. "They're all screwed up—every one of them—but that's the real story. Joe Buttafuoco, he loves all this. He's a media mongrel. He deserves everything he gets."

Not every media outlet pounced on the story. Joey's hometown newspaper, the *Massapequa Post,* skipped it entirely. At an editorial meeting a few days after Amy's arrest, the staff decided the local school board elections took precedence. This year, a bitter race was brewing between the incumbent school board president and his opponent. Not only that, Farmingdale library and school board candidates were planning to speak at a candidates forum, sponsored by the PTA.

The *Post,* its editor explained later, had its priorities.

So did *Newsday*, the Long Island newspaper. Its priority was to dig up anything it could on Amy Fisher and Joey Buttafuoco. To that end one of its reporters even joined Future Physique, plunking down the four-month $99 membership just a few weeks after the shooting. Paul signed up the woman but made his position clear.

"I'm not discussing Amy anymore, if that's the reason you're joining," he warned the reporter.

"I'm not," the woman insisted. "I really need to get in shape."

Over the next few weeks the reporter called several times, asking whether Amy had contacted Paul from jail. The gym owner patiently reiterated his position: he would not discuss Amy.

The reporter finally gave up. Then she called once more. "Look, I want my money back," she said curtly. "I haven't gone even once to your gym."

Paul explained Future Physique's policy: no refunds. He offered to extend the reporter's membership, free of charge. The reporter was not pleased.

"I can't believe you're ripping me off," she snapped. "I'm coming down there tonight and I want my money refunded." She slammed down the phone.

The reporter never did show up, but a few weeks later, when Amy was released on bail, she called Paul again.

"I hope there's no hard feelings between us," she said, her voice all sugary. "I hear Amy's first stop is the gym."

Now it was Paul's turn to slam down the phone.

Chapter
Nineteen

With the media spotlight on a variety of new characters, Joey Buttafuoco was feeling a bit left out. He still chatted gamely with reporters camped on his front lawn—he even passed out sandwiches one afternoon. But slowly Joey was beginning to realize he didn't exactly look great in this imbroglio. It was time to tell his side of the tale, his version of the Amy affair.

That he chose to speak out at length came as no surprise. It was the forum he selected—Howard Stern's radio show—that confounded Joey's supporters and critics alike.

Shortly after 7:00 A.M. on Friday, June 5, Joey turned the dial on his kitchen radio to his favorite early morning show—WXRK, 92.3 FM—home of shock-rock host Howard Stern. Joey began slicing salami for his children's lunch boxes. Mary Jo lay in bed, her head aching. Paul and Jessica dressed hurriedly and packed books and pencils for school.

It wasn't unusual for Stern's baritone to echo through the Buttafuoco home. Joey loved his show. Every morning from 6:00 A.M. to 10:00 A.M. Stern tested the limits of decency and propriety. His controversial humor trashed gays, blacks, Jews, women—a veritable free-for-all of raucous barbs. Some mornings Stern offered complimentary concert tickets to women who appeared at his studio and showed him their breasts. He held butt bongo contests. Occasionally he discussed the size of his genitals.

On this morning, as Joey helped his children get ready for school, the repairman listened to Stern's show more intently than ever. On the air, Stern was gossiping with a man who said he had been Joey Buttafuoco's landscaper. Not only had he seen Amy Fisher at the Buttafuoco home, said the caller, he'd even caught Joey and Amy romping naked in the swimming pool.

Joey was indignant. He didn't even own a swimming pool. It was time, he decided, to speak out publicly. He picked up the phone and dialed WXRK.

A few minutes after he identified himself, Joey Buttafuoco was on the air. Editors of the New York tabloids tuned in to the show began envisioning the next day's cover story. At Channel 12 on Long Island, a quick-thinking studio technician turned a camera on the radio and caught most of the interview. Stern fans were captivated. This was better than lesbian dial-a-date.

For the next ten minutes Joey chatted happily with his favorite radio host, their conversation punctuated with good-natured ribbing and lots of laughter. Joey complained about all the housework he'd been doing since Mary Jo had been shot. He said he'd been getting better at dealing with the press. He added that his wife was better, but in a lot of pain.

Then he casually dropped the bombshell, startling even the imperious Howard Stern. Joey said he had not been unfaithful to his wife. Never, he insisted, had he had an affair with Amy Fisher. As Stern continued to press him, Buttafuoco repeatedly answered, "Absolutely not."

Joey Buttafuoco's denial of the affair came as a complete surprise. For more than two weeks the media—from *The New York Times* to "A Current Affair"—had quoted detectives who said Joey had admitted having a sexual relationship with Amy Fisher. Neither Joey nor his lawyer, Michael Rindenow, the Buttafuocos' old family friend, had ever disputed the allegations to the press.

Choosing Howard Stern's radio show to deny the affair seemed bizarre. Joey's Biltmore Shores neighbors were embarrassed. At Nassau County Police Headquarters in Mineola, detectives were incredulous. In Happauge, Amy Fisher's lawyer, Eric Naiburg, laughed. Joey Buttafuoco was now denying the affair? On the Howard Stern show?

With his wife convalescing in enormous pain, Joey's lighthearted banter with Howard Stern struck New Yorkers as unfeeling and immature. Within days Joey apologized, saying it was a mistake to call Stern. But by then the impression had stuck. Downing coffee and driving to work, thousands of East Coast Howard Stern fans listened to an exchange that was hard to believe.

HOWARD: You know, I had a feeling you'd be a listener.

JOEY: I'm definitely a listener. . . .

HOWARD: How is your wife feeling?

JOEY: Mary Jo is feeling a little better, man. She really can't do much for herself. I'm doing everything, bathing her, doing her hair. Whatever she did, man, I'm doing. Like I couldn't afford to pay her to do what she does, I'm telling you, man.

HOWARD: Let me tell you something. I feel guilty about my wife when I don't do stuff? You've got to be the guiltiest husband in the world.

JOEY: No, I'm not guilty.

HOWARD: You've got to be riddled with guilt.

JOEY: Nooo.

ROBIN: Why not?

JOEY: Why not? Because I have never in my life with her minimized what she has done.

ROBIN: But we're talking about what *you've* done.

HOWARD: Wait till she realizes you were cheating on her. She's going to kill you.

JOEY: Howard. I wasn't cheatin' on my wife. That's a good question, Howard. (*Laughs*) I was faithful to my wife.

HOWARD: Really?

JOEY: Yes.

ROBIN: So this stuff in the press is a lie?

JOEY: Robin? Very nice to talk to you this morning, too. (*Laughs*).

ROBIN: I know. I've just been calling you names all morning. . . .

ROBIN: Are you into that "deny at all costs?" Is that your mode? . . .

JOEY: I can't believe you guys are trying to bury me this morning. *(Laughs)* I'm telling you . . . I'm just taking it a day at a time.

HOWARD: Meanwhile the gardener says Amy used to be over your house. Is that true?

Laughter.

JOEY: That's insane.

HOWARD: Really.

JOEY: Yeah. When my kids heard that report, where she claims to have said my kids call her Aunt Amy? My son, who's twelve, went nuts. He's twelve and he talks like I talk, you know what I'm saying? He'd give me everything from A to Z on how wrong that was.

HOWARD: So you're claiming that the papers are lying when they call you Amy's lover.

JOEY: Absolutely yes.

HOWARD: Wow.

JOEY: You're getting a first, Howard.

ROBIN: Well, then I'm sorry for everything I've said about you.

JOEY: Well, thank you, Robin. *(Laughter)*

ROBIN: I guess that yearbook stuff was true.

HOWARD: You really do love Mary Jo.

JOEY: Absolutely. Absolutely. She's my high school sweetheart. I've been dying to be with a thirty-seven-year-old girl all my life. I finally got one. What the hell am I going to go back to a sixteen- or seventeen-year-old throwback?

ROBIN: This is a good defense. I like this.

HOWARD: I like this. Listen, whether this is true or not, I would stick with this. I would be in complete denial. *(Laughter)*

JOEY: It's just how I feel, Howard. It's where I'm at in my life right today.

HOWARD: In other words, it's not like, "In my mind I've always loved my wife, but even though physically . . ."

ROBIN: "So I strayed a little bit. . . ."

JOEY: I have a very beautiful wife.

HOWARD: You're saying you are clean as a whistle.

JOEY: Yes.

HOWARD: In all of this.

JOEY: Absolutely.

ROBIN: So why did she shoot your wife?

JOEY: Let me just tell you what happen. She comes to the front door of my house. Rings the bell. Okay? . . . Some kind of a dialogue goes down. My wife ended it, turned to go into the house—

HOWARD: I wonder what they were talking about.

JOEY: Um . . . I really can't get into that part of it, Howard, right now.

HOWARD: That's all right. I'm a lawyer.

JOEY: You're everything, man. *(Laughs)*

HOWARD: I might need to represent you.

JOEY: I might need you to. *(Laughter)* Let me just tell you this. Mary Jo turned to go into the house. Amy Fisher put a gun to my wife's head,

Howard, and pulled the trigger . . . And it was no accident.

ROBIN: Of course it's no accident.

HOWARD: I don't think it's an accident.

ROBIN: I thought that was the most stupid statement ever made in this whole case.

HOWARD: And you are now claiming that Amy Fisher is totally hallucinating that she had a relationship with you?

JOEY: Yes.

ROBIN: But you know her, right?

JOEY: Through business only at my repair shop. It was her father, we did work for her dad.

ROBIN: How did she become obsessed with you? This is an odd thing.

JOEY: Uhh. I just—

HOWARD: This is what I would say. "Hey, sees me at the car place, she falls in love with me in her mind."

JOEY: I guess so, Howard.

HOWARD: I like this defense.

JOEY: I mean, I see a lot of people every day. I mean, I see a lot of people.

ROBIN: Well, your wife better hide. You're so incredible they just fall in love with you.

HOWARD: You know what it is? If this is true, you are so attractive, you must have huge balls or something.

JOEY: You know, I was wondering when you were going to start that. *(Laughs)*

HOWARD: You say you are so attractive that really . . . What is it, your face?

JOEY: Come on now. Be nice. *(Laughs)* Be nice.

HOWARD: And your wife's buying all this. Right?

JOEY: It's not a matter of buying. . . . We have a very trusting relationship. We're really close. As I say, those who know us—

ROBIN: I can't even tell you what they're saying about you in beauty shops around town.

HOWARD: Now when will you come in here so I can hook you up to a lie detector test?

JOEY: Think I'll need dial-a-date, Howard? *(Laughs)*

HOWARD: Yeah, I think so. We'll put you on dial-a-date.

JOEY: Oh, no no. *(Laughs)*

HOWARD: You don't need dial-a-date. Evidently you walk down the street women are attracted to you.

JOEY: Oh, come on now. Be nice to me. Hey, huh?

HOWARD: Well, I am being nice.

JOEY: It's the one thing. I haven't talked to anyone.

HOWARD: I've been very nice.

JOEY: You have. You've been great. *(Laughs)*

HOWARD: I really have. I could be a lot worse.

ROBIN: I'm very sorry for what happened to your wife.

HOWARD: Yeah. We feel bad for your wife.

JOEY: Thank you.

ROBIN: And your whole family.

JOEY: Yeah. My son's breaking my chops. I got to get him to school.

HOWARD: What's the deal, man? At school the kids must be driving him nuts.

JOEY: Actually not. We're in a great school over here. He's going to a school that I went to as a kid over here in Massapequa. So it's like, you know, I go there and see some teachers I had, and they were fossils when *I* went to school. *(Laughter)* But it's a good school and my kids are great.

,HOWARD: Buttafooooo is an unusual name.

JOEY: It's Buttafuoco.

HOWARD: Fuoco, it's a very unusual name. Buttafuoco. What does that mean in Italian?

JOEY: Thrower of fire.

HOWARD: Thrower of fire. Well, so far that hasn't happened . . . All right. Check in with us as this progresses. *(Laughter)*

JOEY: You got it, Howard.

HOWARD: Joe Buttafuoco, ladies and gentlemen. *(Laughter)*

ROBIN: Well, shut my mouth.

HOWARD: Yeah, well, guy says he didn't know her? Well, what do you know? Who knows?

ROBIN: I guess I have to take back everything I said.

HOWARD: Well, I don't know if you have to do that. I don't know about that.

ROBIN: You don't believe him?

HOWARD: No. *(Laughs)* I think I'd do the same thing.

ROBIN: It's a great defense.

HOWARD: But I would do the same exact thing. Wait a minute, let me think about this for a second. Nobody knows what I was up to. . . . "I never met this girl." That's what I would tell my wife. Damn right. She's laying [sic] there with bandages on her head, you're damn sure. And then you're taking care of the kids and have to do everything. You go. Wait a second, this is a lot of work. This is a lot of work. I could never admit that. . . .

Silence.

HOWARD: I'll tell you. This guy is wild. I knew he was a listener. As soon as I saw this on the news. I knew Amy Fisher was a listener. I knew her neighbors were listeners. I knew for sure he was a listener.

ROBIN: Oh, sure. These are our people.

HOWARD: Oh, yeah. I definitely know he listens every morning. And Mrs. Buttafuoco probably thinks we're disgusting. I got to tell you something. Whether it's true or not, that's a fabulous defense.

ROBIN: Well, you know. If he took the stand, do you think they could break him down? We couldn't break him.

HOWARD: No. If we can't break him, nobody can. All right. Very good. We'll come back right after these words.

The show broke for a commercial. Stern and Quivers sat back in amazement. The phone lines lit up as reporters appealed for permission to run a tape of the interview on the evening news. A reporter from Channel 12, the local Long Island station, was first. The station, the woman said, was "mesmerized" by the exchange.

Stern loved it. Back on the air, he quickly issued his demands. Anyone interested in using a tape of the interview must negotiate directly with him—on the air—and agree to give him the following credit: Howard Stern, King of Media.

On that day Howard Stern deserved it. The interview rocketed Joey Buttafuoco back to the front pages of the New York dailies. JOEY SAYS IT AIN'T SO, read the *New York Post*. AMY WHO? nudged *Newsday*. From the *Daily News*, JOEY UNZIPS LIP TO SING A NEW TUNE.

Howard Stern wasn't finished with the Joey Buttafuoco/Amy Fisher imbroglio. Later that morning a former employee of Complete Auto Body called in to say Joey's denial of an affair with Amy was a lie. At Stern's request the caller a few days later brought in a pay stub from the auto body shop to prove he had worked there.

CALLER: Exactly what he had told me: that he gave her her first orgasm and that basically drove her wild and that's what made her so infatuated with him. I hid him in a customer's Blazer one day in the back while she was looking for him up front. She was pacing back and forth in the front of the shop frantically looking for him. That's when he told me about it. . . . Mary Jo is a real sweet person. And I've told him right to his face I don't care for the way he treats her. He's a lot of bunk, saying he loves her. He does love his children, you know, and I seriously doubt he would have anything to do with his wife being shot. He wouldn't take the mother from his children.

HOWARD: Now, did his wife know about Amy?

CALLER: No, she did not. The whole shop knew about it. There's no doubt about that. I know Joey personally and I know him well. I happen to know half the hookers in North Freeport know him by name. . . . I will swear in a court of law on a stack of Bibles. I wish he would call right now, because he would recognize my voice.

The caller may very well get his chance to speak in court. A few weeks after that radio exchange he was interviewed by investigators for the defense. He may be called to testify at Amy's trial about the affair.

The Howard Stern contretemps was a media boon, but for Joey Buttafuoco it was a personal disaster. Later that morning, detectives from Nassau County's homicide division called him, irritated.

"Are you crazy?" one said. "You're a target for everybody in this thing. Everybody hates you. And now they're really going to hate you."

In the wake of the media fuss, Joey also lost his attorney, Michael Rindenow. The long-term friend of the Buttafuocos had been busy for weeks handling the press, arranging a civil suit against Amy Fisher and her parents, and negotiating a movie deal. Juggling the Buttafuocos' needs and his regular clients wasn't easy. When he learned of Joey's chat with Howard Stern, Rindenow felt betrayed. He had frequently reminded the repairman not to talk about the case.

Rindenow didn't hear the radio show that morning, but he found out about it fast. Immediately after the interview was broadcast, Rindenow took a call from the producer of a rival radio station.

"What happened?" the producer said, disappointed. "You promised us first dibs at Joey Buttafuoco on radio."

"What are you talking about?"

"Joey was on Howard Stern's radio show this morning."

"You've got to be kidding me."

Rindenow couldn't believe it. He hung up, then picked up the phone to call Joey. The phone rang again. It was a reporter.

"How could you let your client go on Howard Stern?" the reporter asked.

"I had no idea about any of this." Rindenow sighed. "I told him not to speak to anyone. I'm going to call him right now."

When Rindenow finally got Joey on the line, the repairman was penitent.

"Did you hear about my dumb move?" Joey said.

"Yes, I heard about your dumb move," Rindenow shot back. "Joey, I can't continue to represent you if you're going to do things like that. I'm not going to be your lawyer if you're not going to listen to me."

"Mike, I'm sorry, but the things they were saying . . . They had this gardener on, saying I was in the pool with Amy and Mary Jo. Mike, I looked out my window, I don't even have a pool. I lost it."

"Joey, I'm going to call someone else in on this. You need another attorney."

The next day Rindenow contacted Marvyn Kornberg. The Queens attorney, flashy and glib, was an expert in criminal defense and one of Rindenow's longtime friends. The two talked at length that weekend and met Monday morning for a strategy session.

It was decided that Rindenow would continue to represent Mary Jo. Kornberg would handle any criminal charges that might be leveled at Joey.

With Kornberg at his side, Joey was finally restrained. In his first post-Stern interview, Joey tried to explain his radio blunder. "Hey, I've only been doing this fourteen days," he said. "I'm sorry. It won't happen again."

Chapter Twenty

Other radio stations enjoyed the conundrum just as much. On WPLJ, 95.5 FM, deejays Scott Shannon and Todd Pettingill discussed movie possibilities for the Amy/Joey story. Drew Barrymore, Pettingill insisted, as Amy. "That's a lock," he quipped.

Shannon mocked Joey Buttafuoco's denial of the affair. " 'I had nothing to do with it,' " he said, imitating Joey. " 'I don't even know this girl. She just came in to get her car repaired. . . . Ten times. . . . Always breaking down.' By the way, when I was sixteen and I crashed my parents' car I wasn't the person who drove it into the garage. After I got my head handed to me on a platter Dad took the car into the shop. I wasn't the one who always went into the repair shop. On top of it all, the guy calls Howard Stern to explain his position. Even his lawyers were doing the Edward Kennedy slow burn. 'No, no.' I was never so happy in all my life that Howard Stern had a listener when this guy called."

Howard Stern wasn't the only radio personality to host a conversation with a member of Mary Jo Buttafuoco's family: early one morning, about three weeks after the shooting, WOR's "Rambling with Gambling" show got a surprise call-in from Patricia Connery, Mary Jo's mom.

A news assistant took the call just after 7:00 A.M. It was the usual busy morning on the phone lines when a woman called to say her name was Patricia Connery, the mother of Mary Jo Buttafuoco. She was tired of listening to everyone trash her son-in-law, Joey. She wanted New Yorkers to know she loved him and supported him completely.

Following procedure, the assistant asked for Connery's phone number and called her back. Researchers then scrambled through Cole's Directory, which arranges names in order of telephone numbers, trying to verify the call was indeed coming from the Connery home in Massapequa Park. As the radio show went to a commercial, host John Gambling took the call, asking the woman a few questions. In minutes he was satisfied she was indeed Mary Jo's mother and put her on the air.

CONNERY: Good morning, John.

GAMBLING: Now you have seen the newspapers this morning. For example, AMY OFFERED SEX FOR MURDER, is one headline. . . .

CONNERY: No, I haven't. I do very little of reading the newspapers. I just don't have the energy to push through anger. I have to save my energy for Mary Jo, for Joe, the children, my whole family. I kind of gave up reading the papers.

GAMBLING: Okay. I can maybe understand that, but you know what's going on. You know what's being said. First of all, how is Mary Jo physically?

CONNERY: Mary Jo is in a tremendous amount of pain. She still has double vision. She still has tremendous amount of problems with her ear, can't hear. What the results are, we don't know. What the end results are going to be . . . But the thing is, she's in pain twenty-four hours a day. She has to go for all kinds of therapy. Like yesterday they [the media] caught Joe taking her out, and that was because she was going for therapy. As I said to you earlier I called you because I know you're not a sleazy program, and you're not a sleazy media. And this is why I just felt I had to say something in favor of my family and her family. And as I told you before, John, and I will say it again, I will lay down my life for my son-in-law. And they'll have to go through me to get to him.

GAMBLING: You don't buy any of this.

CONNERY: None of it. Absolutely none of it. I have known him since he was sixteen years old, and he is my son. I don't consider him my son-in-law. He is my son. He's one of my kids.

GAMBLING: Now, I know you are limited in what you will say and can say about all this, but you have talked to Joseph Buttafuoco about the events and the allegations.

CONNERY: Yes.

GAMBLING: And after hearing all those things, you're still not buying into any of what's been said.

CONNERY: Not one iota. Not one bit.

GAMBLING: And Mary Jo, her attitude. The same?

CONNERY: Exactly the same. They're devoted to each other. That's all I can tell you.

GAMBLING: Do you know Amy Fisher?

CONNERY: Absolutely not. I never met her until I saw her face on the news that day. I don't know anything about it. I have to say my heart goes out to her parents. It must be awful, just terrible.

GAMBLING: Well, it's an ordeal for you and your family as well.

CONNERY: Well, of course. But I pray for her and her family as much as my own.

GAMBLING: And how about your neighborhood, your community? How are they reacting?

CONNERY: They have been the most wonderful, supportive neighbors, friends, you could ever imagine. They're behind them, they're behind us. They are just wonderful.

GAMBLING: We're talking to Mary Jo Buttafuoco's mother, Pat on the "Rambling with Gambling" telephone this morning here. Where do you think this will go?

CONNERY: I don't really know. I just hope the nightmare gets over soon, 'cause you wake up every morning thinking it's a bad dream and then you know it isn't. I just pray and hope and I hope the whole nation keeps praying for Mary Jo because she needs a lot of prayer, and Joe, that they can hold up under all of this. *(Laughs)* My youngest daughter's adding not such nice words we can't use on the radio in the background. She just said to me, "I just hope someday, Mom, I could find a guy like Joe." That's my youngest daughter. I don't know what else to tell you. I had to put a stop as much as I could to all of this, and just fight for him.

GAMBLING: But you know every day the allegations coming from the police department, from the lawyer's offices, other places. It's getting worse and worse rather than better and better.

CONNERY: Oh, sure. We knew it would. I mean, that's news. Does anybody want to read anything? . . . You think anyone's going to listen to what I just said? Nah. That's not newsworthy. That's truth, honesty. We have so much love and so much honesty around us. We're surrounded by it. Nobody can hurt us. They can't. They just can't hurt us.

GAMBLING: How's your daughter making out? She's got to exist in her community, in her society, in her world. . . .

CONNERY: The worst is yet to come because she is very, very fearful. Very fearful. I guess as any one of us would be if we lived a normal suburban life all our lives and never expected anything like this to happen.

GAMBLING: No, no, even in your worst nightmare.

CONNERY: No, no.

GAMBLING: How do you think this got started?

CONNERY: As I said, I can't comment on that because I don't know. I called you to defend my family because I love my family and I love my son-in-law.

GAMBLING: Pat, I hope that you will allow me to call you back as things develop and maybe we can talk some more. I think your perspective on this, being the mother of Mary Jo Buttafuoco, certainly is one of interest because I think we all at one time or another will put ourselves in other people's positions in stories we read about and wonder how we would react. So if we can strengthen this trust between each other, I might have the opportunity to call you back again.

CONNERY: I'd like that, John. I really would. And I would have no qualms with you calling me anytime.

GAMBLING: Pat, thank you very much.

CONNERY: Thank you for giving me this opportunity.

Pat Connery hung up the phone, a bit unsteady. She took a deep breath. There. She'd done it. Told thousands of New Yorkers loud and clear. On Biltmore Boulevard, Caspar Buttafuoco was pleased: he'd heard the program as he got ready for work. Many of Pat Connery's friends and neighbors had listened as well.

Pat worried that a flood of reporters would suddenly show up to her home, but overall she was pleased with herself. Later that morning she talked to Joey and told him what she'd said. "You're something, Ma," he said with a laugh.

The next morning Caspar Buttafuoco spoke out as well, defending his youngest son in a phone interview with *Newsday* columnist Dennis Duggan. From his desk at Complete Auto Body, the elderly man asserted that Joey was getting a raw deal.

"If I thought my son was guilty even one iota, I'd gladly send the sonavabitch to hell and let him burn for eternity," he said earnestly. "I love my son, and it's really rough to have to sit here and listen to all these lies about him. It makes my blood boil, but I've been told to keep my mouth shut. I wish I could tell you what the real story here is. That girl makes poison ivy look good. I'll tell you this: I will go to hell and back for this boy because he is one hundred percent right. If he wasn't, I'd let him suffer by himself."

Foremost in her mind was her fear of Amy Fisher.

"What if they let her out on bail?" she often said tearfully. "She's going to kill me. She's going to finish me off."

The family tried to reassure Mary Jo. Police had promised to patrol the area exhaustively, and the Buttafuocos, too, would consider hiring their own security guards. Mary Jo, they vowed, would be protected.

Eleven days after the .25-caliber bullet tore into her skull, Mary Jo waved good-bye to the nurses and doctors who had helped save her life. At last she was going home. Leaning on her husband and bracing herself with a cane, she hobbled past throngs of reporters lining Adam Road West. Photographers shot entire rolls of film in minutes. Reporters shouted questions. Neighbors honked car horns and called out greetings.

Later that afternoon Michael Rindenow and his wife dropped by to welcome Mary Jo home.

"I can't believe all this," she told them. "Everything you were telling me was right. All this attention. What do they think, I'm a movie star?"

The fuss over Mary Jo's homecoming didn't die down for weeks. She began going for daily physical therapy at the hospital. Every morning photographers loitered in the road by the Buttafuocos' driveway, hoping to catch Mary Jo walking sluggishly to the car. For a while, the *New York Daily News* assigned a photographer to stake out One Adam Road West full-time.

During hour sessions in the hospital, physical

therapists put electrical prods into the right side of her face and stimulated the area continually for at least half an hour. Since her facial nerves are not working properly, the muscle tissue that surrounds them deteriorates from lack of movement. With the electrical current forcing the muscles to move, they may stay healthy. When Mary Jo emerges from therapy, her face is bright red.

In the future she may undergo surgery to graft a nerve from another part of her body to her face. To meet with specialists once a week, she and Joey battle traffic on the Long Island Expressway and travel some forty miles to Manhattan for appointments at Mt. Sinai Medical Center. The trip is draining on Mary Jo.

But the housewife tries to remain optimistic. If a nerve graft succeeds, she may regain sensation on the right side of her face. She tries not to think about complications. Nerve graft success depends on many factors, including how much scar tissue remains in the area. If nerves begin to grow but encounter scar tissue, growth often stops abruptly.

Except for physical therapy, Mary Jo seldom left her bed in those first few weeks at home. In the mornings Joey bathed her, fixed her hair, and helped her dress. At night he cooked meat and potatoes and pureed it through a blender. Propped up in bed, Mary Jo sipped dinner through a straw. Once, bleary from exhaustion, Mary Jo asked for a McDonald's Big Mac.

She has endured troubling setbacks. At home

one day in Massapequa, she doubled over, complaining of severe stomach pains. Joey called 911, and police sent an ambulance at once. Back at Nassau County Medical Center, doctors determined that Mary Jo had suffered an adverse reaction to medication. They admitted her overnight and ran tests. She was also treated for an inner-ear infection.

The daily drive to the hospital for therapy often touched off uncomfortable feelings as well. Mary Jo shuddered to recall that the Nassau County Correctional Facility was just a few blocks from the medical center. Behind its iron gates was the auburn-haired girl with the T-shirt—the girl wielding the .25-caliber Titan that nearly destroyed her life. Mary Jo frequently dissolved into tears whenever she glanced in the jail's direction.

"I don't understand why this happened," she'd say weakly. "When is this all going to end?"

Sometimes Mary Jo wonders if it ever will.

To combat her fears, Mary Jo decided to face her assailant. About a month after the shooting, she picked Amy Fisher out of a police lineup. For days the family's attorneys, Rindenow and Kornberg, had flatly told her not to participate. It wasn't necessary, they insisted. Besides, if for some reason she couldn't identify Amy, there might be problems at the trial. But Assistant District Attorney Fred Klein disagreed. He dropped by the Buttafuoco home one evening, trying to persuade the Massapequa housewife that he needed her identification to present the prosecution's case.

Mary Jo didn't do it for the case: she did it for herself. She was determined to confront the young woman who had caused her such suffering. On the morning of the lineup, she and Joey were driven to police headquarters in a black car with tinted windows, entering through an underground garage. Disappointed reporters and photographers only glimpsed the car speeding by.

Upstairs, in a darkened room, Mary Jo stiffened as she stepped up to the one-way mirror and gazed into the viewing room, flooded with light. She looked carefully at the faces of each of the six girls standing motionless, their bodies covered by white sheets. For a long time she stared at the third girl from the right. Then, softly, she spoke.

"It's number three," she said.

A homicide detective nodded. Number three was Amy Fisher, he told her.

Mary Jo Buttafuoco began to cry. Hugging her husband, she asked to go home. When they pulled into the driveway of One Adam Road West, Mary Jo went directly to bed with the worst headache she'd ever had.

In her first exclusive interview, with Mike McAlary, a columnist for the *New York Post*, Mary Jo described her physical condition. "I feel about forty percent of what I was," she said. "I've had major surgery. They had to open me up. I've lost a lot of blood. I'm fatigued. If I do anything physical, even to stand up and walk across the room, it's a chore. I have to lie down and rest. I'm glad to be home, but I'm still in a lot of pain. Mostly what I feel is pain."

Some of the pain is emotional. She becomes agitated when she reads the aspersions leveled at her husband. Mary Jo has made it clear that her marriage is sturdy and unharmed by what has happened. She has a husband she loves and trusts.

"I'm standing behind Joey," she said. "I believe in Joey. We have a wonderful marriage. Our relationship has never been a problem. We're more together now than ever because of all that has happened. My recovery is being hampered by the horrible things that people are saying. My Joey, the things that they're saying about him are terrible. What has happened has made me furious. Absolutely furious.

"There are all these people running around with stories—people that don't know anything about us or our lives. All of these people are telling stories from the 'inside.' Only Joey and I know the inside story. And the story is pretty simple: I love my Joey. My Joey loves me. Nothing that has happened to me—or will happen in this case—has changed that. We're forever. We're not just husband and wife. We're lifelong friends. We're real friends. We know everything there is to know about each other. We haven't had a fairy-tale life. But who does? We have disagreements just like everyone else. And now all these things are being written and said. Cheating. Infidelity. The things that have been reported are lies. We've had our difficulties. What married couple out there hasn't? I don't blame Joey for any of this. No one else should, either."

Chapter
Twenty-Two

Once Amy's bail was set at $2 million, hope of bringing her home before trial dimmed. When Elliot and Rose Fisher added up every cent they had—about $584,000 in liquid assets and the house, valued at $400,000—it reached barely half the amount they needed.

Two days after the hearing, Eric Naiburg pressed a four-judge panel at the appellate division of the state supreme court in Brooklyn to lower the $2 million bail. He cited a number of recent high-profile cases where the crimes were worse but the bail lower. He asked that Amy's bail be reduced to a $250,000 bond or $50,000 cash. "This is a typical teenager who needs to be home with her family preparing for high school graduation," he told them.

Fred Klein's rebuttal was sharp. This woman, he insisted, was no typical teenager. She was a manipulative prostitute who'd probably disappear shortly after she walked out of jail. "She could slide into that sleazy world and no one would be able to find her, and she could support herself very well," Klein said. "She's as dangerous as John Gotti. . . . The Buttafuoco family is petrified you will release this girl."

Klein's argument was convincing. Within a few hours the judges issued a terse written decision without explanation: "The application is denied and the writ is dismissed."

Naiburg called Amy to break the news, arranging a conference call with her mother on the line as well. When told bail remained at $2 million, Amy began to cry.

"Hang in there tight," Naiburg said. "I'm still working on this."

Amy's parents were also crushed. They'd had high hopes for the appeal. Rose Fisher hung up the phone in tears. "How can this be?" she kept asking. "How can this be happening?"

Chris Edwards-Neumann held her hand. "A runaway train is like that," she said. "It doesn't stop for red lights, it doesn't stop for yellow lights, and it doesn't stop for green lights. Once they called this 'fatal attraction' the train took off. I've never seen a case like this."

In Massapequa Joey was busy giving interviews on his front lawn. He was pleased the bail reduction was denied, but the repairman was quick to deny any animosity toward Amy. "I don't hate Amy Fisher," he explained. "I think she needs a tremendous amount of help. She's got a lot of excess baggage up in that head of hers."

* * *

For Eric Naiburg, Amy's inability to make bail was injurious to her defense. The teenager's emotional state was deteriorating. She barely ate, and when she did manage to choke down food, she promptly threw up. She slept little and cried for hours in her jail cot. At times on the telephone, she sounded almost incoherent.

Naiburg tried to keep her spirits up, but his own were dashed. He didn't know what else to do. One night at home in Dix Hills, Long Island, Naiburg talked about the case to his daughters, Jennifer and Marnie.

"What can I do?" he said. "How can I get her out? She has no assets."

He stopped. Amy did have an important asset: her story. The Merrick teenager was the hottest topic in town. She'd been on the front page of the New York City newspapers for almost three weeks. Her cavorting on the "Current Affair" tapes had made her story national as well.

Eric Naiburg took a controversial step. He offered the exclusive rights to Amy's story in return for the $2 million bail. At a press conference he announced he was seeking the entire bail, which would be refundable if Amy appeared for trial, or a bail bondsman's nonrefundable fee of $100,000. Unspoken was the risk the would-be story buyer must take: if Amy Fisher did not appear in court, the buyer would be liable for $2 million.

Within a few days Naiburg was inundated with calls from Hollywood moviemakers, television networks, and well-known actors. He outlined his terms: Amy and her parents would be available for an exclusive interview, but only after trial. No information divulged could hurt Amy's defense, and Naiburg himself must be a participant to any interviews. He began to negotiate other terms, including the possibility of a round-the-clock security guard to make sure Amy didn't run.

It was a provocative idea. Yet it seemed far-fetched. Movie rights seldom sold for more than $100,000—certainly not $2 million. The defendant often didn't even get paid for rights: in most cases, once a case went to trial a transcript could provide any of the action a script writer needed. In Amy's case, many studios were reluctant to get involved in a criminal case.

Yet Naiburg insisted he had twenty offers and had winnowed it down to seven after consulting with entertainment lawyers and Amy's parents. He said it was simply a matter of first come, first served. Amy, he told the press, would probably be home by the end of the week.

The media went agog with the story. COAST IN LOVE WITH AMY. LET'S DO LUNCH, NOT TIME, SAY "20," headlined the *Daily News*. The *Post* was equally upbeat: HOLLYWOOD BIGS ARE LINING UP TO INK AMY: LAWYER. *Newsday* took a more cynical view: HOW SLEAZY CAN THIS STORY GET?

Naiburg's offbeat idea took the district attorney's office by surprise. Fred Klein began exploring ways to circumvent it. He could ask for higher or no bail by adding charges—perhaps premeditation, now that he had testimony from Stephen Sleeman. Or he could argue there was a good chance Amy would bolt, unconcerned if a movie studio lost $2 million. He requested that the court and jail notify him if Amy's bail was posted. He planned to ask immediately for a sufficiency hearing to examine the assets being posted. He hoped a judge would find the assets to be inadequate. Then Amy would remain behind bars.

A legal battle over Amy's assets began stirring as well. Joe Buttafuoco's attorney lashed out, saying he would sue Amy Fisher for any money she received for her story. That money, Marvyn Kornberg thundered, should go to the Buttafuocos.

Was bail money part of a defendant's assets? Legal experts began debating the issue. To make matters more complicated, the New York State Senate unanimously passed a revised "Son of Sam" law the same week Naiburg announced the deal for Amy's rights. The 1977 Son of Sam Law, named for the serial killer, restricted criminals and those under indictment from profiting from their crimes by selling their stories. Simon & Schuster had sued to overturn the law, taking its case all the way to the United States Supreme Court. The book company published a book on mob informant Henry Hill, written by Nicholas Pileggi. The book became the film *Goodfellas*, starring Robert De Niro and Joe Pesci.

In December the Supreme Court overturned the Son of Sam Law, ruling that the law violated the First Amendment.

Under the new law, victims of crimes would be

able to lay claim to at least a portion of any profits by the criminal over a longer period of time. It didn't prevent the criminal from making a profit but made it easier for crime victims to collect, increasing the statute of limitations on claims to ten years from one year.

In the days that followed his announcement, Naiburg fended off criticism and attempted to clarify his proposal. In his office he held a press conference. "Usually people in this situation—the Mike Tysons and the Kennedys—have signifianct financial assets of their own," he said. "Amy Fisher happens to be a high school student. Her only asset is her story."

As he turned to go into his office, a television newscaster asked him if maybe this whole thing didn't look a little sleazy.

"I don't know why you think this is a bad thing," Naiburg snapped. "I'm trying to get this child out of jail. The only one who can't post bail is me, because of ethics. She's not making a penny on this. Neither am I."

The newscaster backed off.

Naiburg, annoyed, settled behind his cluttered desk for yet another interview. On the floor by the door lay the worn brown folder he used to file papers. On top he'd jotted down phone numbers—Amy's parents, Fred Klein's home and office phone, the jail, and John Esposito. The reporter who spotted these numbers was puzzled. The name Esposito had not yet appeared in the press. John Esposito would turn out to be the lawyer for Peter Guagenti. Interestingly, no one would hear the name of the mystery driver for two more weeks.

Eric Naiburg began to talk. He'd done this ritual dozens of times already and knew it well. "Amy Fisher was used and abused by Mr. Buttafuoco," he said. "This man, twenty years her senior, did a number of things that were reprehensible, including putting a young girl into prostitution and using her for his own purposes. I believe the wrong person stands before the docket at this time. I have offered Amy's exclusive story so she can get out of jail and help us participate in her defense. It will make my job a lot easier. It's kind of unique, but I don't think a case has ever had this kind of publicity."

Amy, he said, was distraught but holding up. "Amy is a tough little kid. She gets knocked down every once in a while, but she comes back up. I'm proud of her. I tell her not to read the press and not to watch television, but she does."

What about Joe Buttafuoco's chat with Howard Stern? If Naiburg had the proof of the affair, hadn't the auto repairman shot himself in the foot?

Naiburg grinned. He leaned forward. "Higher," he hissed.

"Excuse me?" the reporter said, puzzled.

"Did he shoot himself in the foot? Higher. He shot himself higher."

The tension eased. Naiburg laughed at his joke and pushed back his chair.

As weeks passed, Eric Naiburg's confident announcement of an imminent deal with a Hollywood knight proved premature. He continued to battle legally to reduce the bail. Before Judge Goodman in Mineola, Naiburg reiterated that Amy was not doing well in jail. Wearing a long-sleeved blue denim shirt and white jeans, Amy listened, looking painfully thin.

Naiburg complained that the women's jail did not have facilities for attorneys to meet privately with clients. He said when he talked to Amy he was forced to meet her in a cavernous visiting room with at least one hundred other prisoners and their families.

"Everybody looks, everybody points, everybody wants to sit next to us and be part of our conversation," he told the judge.

If released, he said, his client would gladly agree to anything the court ordered—house arrest, calling a probation officer twice a day, twenty-four-hour security guard, anything. Amy's parents, he stressed, could afford $1 million bail—every cent they had scraped to save their whole lives.

Judge Goodman was not impressed. Bail remained $2 million.

The same morning Judge Goodman dismissed the appeal, Gambino crime family boss John Gotti was sentenced to life in prison. On the evening news, the Gotti story led the broadcast. Denial of Amy Fisher's bail application was next.

Naiburg tried again, petitioning Supreme Court Justice Kenneth Molloy in Brooklyn. The court was on its summer recess, but at Naiburg's request the justices agreed to reconvene. Naiburg, however, did not give the argument: he asked Thomas Boyle, a Suffolk County appeals specialist, to speak instead.

It was a curious move. Some attorneys speculated that Naiburg sensed the appellate court justices did not like his flamboyant ways. Perhaps if he recruited another attorney to present the case, Amy would benefit.

It was a stifling summer day. Fred Klein arrived at the Monroe Street courtroom early, shuffling through papers in a back room. His assistant disappeared outside to check on the media crunch. He returned laughing. "One lousy camera," he said.

The echo-filled courtroom was practically empty. Rose Fisher and Chris Edwards-Neumann settled into middle-row seats. "Is it okay if we sit here?" Rose asked Naiburg timidly. He motioned for them to move closer, and they did, sitting in the second row. In a folder on her lap, Rose held two five-by-seven pictures of Amy. She and Edwards-Neumann talked quietly.

Naiburg leaned against a desk in the front, reading a copy of *Newsday*. A court officer politely told him to put it away: newspapers were not permitted in the courtroom.

The room fell silent when four black-robed judges entered and took seats at an enormous oak table. Judge Molloy motioned to the defense to present its argument. Thomas Boyle stood and began by thanking the justices for interrupting their vacation to hear the appeal.

"You're welcome, Mr. Boyle," Judge Molloy boomed. "But as they say, 'What's new?' "

Apparently, not much. Boyle gave an argument similar to the one Naiburg had two weeks earlier. Amy, he said, had lost fifteen to twenty pounds and was deteriorating emotionally.

"Those are grounds?" Molloy asked. "Are you suggesting her life is in danger?"

"I think a loss of body weight of almost twenty percent is substantial," Boyle countered.

For a moment there was silence. Boyle moved on quickly. The attorney told the court of poor access to Amy in prison. Just the other day he'd had to wait forty-five minutes in line with prisoners' families before his client was brought by guards into the visiting room. He and Amy talked in whispers, jammed next to other inmates and families, all eyes trained on them.

"There are no private rooms," he said. "There is a blatant violation of women's rights as far as attorney/client privileges are concerned."

"Is she being treated differently from other inmates?" Molloy asked.

No, Boyle admitted, she wasn't.

The attorney concluded by providing a prodigious list of other defendants charged with more serious crimes. Each had received a far lower bail.

Molloy was not swayed. Nothing, he said, was new from the last time Naiburg presented the case. "These are the same arguments," he said sternly. "This same line of argument was made very skillfully by Mr. Naiburg."

Bail reduction was denied. Yet the appeals

ended up having a positive impact on other inmates. A few days after the hearing in Brooklyn, a sign was posted in the women's cell block of the Nassau County Correctional Facility. "Upon request, attorneys may meet with clients in private counseling rooms."

Chapter
Twenty-Three

In jail, Amy quickly gained heroine status. Inmates broke into cheers of "Amy, Amy, Amy" whenever she was led into the visitors room. "Amy" songs and jokes traveled swiftly. Guards were put on notice that any clandestine photographs or videos taken of Long Island's most famous teenager behind bars would mean an automatic dismissal.

Prison officials had reason to be concerned. In 1977 a corrections guard earned thousands of dollars for his snapshot of Son of Sam serial killer David Berkowitz dozing on a prison cot. The *New York Post*'s "Sam Sleeps" cover photo haunted jail officials.

Yet prison guards managed to duck some rules. Several asked Amy for an autograph. Uncomfortable, she complied.

Amy began getting sympathy mail from other prisoners. One letter writer was Daniel Wakefield, a thirty-one-year-old convicted rapist who drew notoriety on Long Island for acting as his own lawyer.

"She looks frail, like she's not eating. She doesn't look good," he told reporters, concerned. "She's the talk of the jail."

In addition to the friendly missives, Amy also got a fair number of obscene ones. Mail also poured in from outside the Nassau County Correctional Facility. The teenager received letters from movie studios, production companies, even struggling actors. One group of would-be thespians, waiters at the Russian Tea Room in Manhattan, sent her a package of their résumés, hoping the teenager might help them land roles in a movie about her life.

Amy tried to ignore the fuss. When male prisoners whistled and chanted her name, she ducked her head and stared at the floor. She didn't pay attention to the "Amy" cartoons or jokes. One was "If polls show Bush and Clinton ahead, Perot and Fisher'll knock 'em dead."

Every day reporters called the jail to ask how Amy was doing and whether she was any trouble at all. Bert Wilson, the former spokesman for the Nassau County Correctional Facility, said the only problems were chronic traffic tie-ups caused by television reporters using the jail's front door as a backdrop for their reports.

The day after her bail was set at $2 million, Amy complained of feeling ill. Prison guards sent for a doctor. The young girl had eaten little in the two weeks since her arrest. She asked for

Kosher meals and began receiving them the same day.

Amy forced herself to eat. She'd lost so much weight that she felt dazed most of the time. Food just didn't seem to stay down. Once, talking with her lawyer in the visitors room, Amy dropped her head to the table, passing out momentarily. When she revived, blood poured from her nose.

Amid the turmoil, Amy took final exams in government and English. She penciled her answers in a room with seven female prisoners taking a high school equivalency exam. It was the first time the prison had given a regents exam. Amy's test was hand-delivered to John F. Kennedy to be graded.

Detectives at police headquarters scoffed at the flurry of media calls. "Is it front-page news that this kid took a test?" one cracked. "Come on."

For the first month of Amy's incarceration she was the only female prisoner on the five-cell youth tier of the women's cell block. Guards woke her at 5:00 A.M. and served breakfast—usually dry toast, juice, and cold cereal. She ate alone in her cell.

Her mother visited as often as permitted—three times weekly—and Amy called home several times a day, collect. She also phoned Naiburg daily, usually after reading the morning newspapers. Joey Buttafuoco's denial of their relationship was bruising. Amy often reread his words in disbelief.

Her family and attorneys encouraged her to read other material—books, magazines, anything to help her pass each day—but Amy seldom did. She watched "Brady Bunch" reruns and traced Disney characters. She wrote letters—mostly to Paul at the gym. "I hope," she wrote in small, neat print, "you don't believe all the things they're saying about me."

Amy also called Paul once or twice a week, usually around 10:00 P.M., when the gym closed.

"Can't you come visit me?" she'd ask. "I think they'll let you in. No one needs to know."

Paul never gave her a direct answer. He wasn't sure he wanted to see her. She sounded so sad on the phone; it made him feel terrible. At the same time he felt a bit cheated. He knew now that Amy had repeatedly lied to him for months, about Joey, the escort service, so many things. He didn't know what happened that morning on Mary Jo Buttafuoco's front stoop, but he did know that Amy Fisher was a lot more mixed up than he'd ever imagined.

Sometimes, on the phone from jail, Amy hinted that she wished things could go back to the way they were before, that they could start over again.

"She's got to be crazy if she thinks I can forget all that's happened," he told a friend.

Still, he wanted to stay in touch with Amy. He asked her a few times about the shooting, but she wouldn't respond. Her lawyer, the teenager said, had made her promise not to talk about the case.

"Okay," Paul said. "Whatever happened, happened. How are you doing?"

"It's boring," she said, sniffling. "But everyone is treating me nice. I just wanted to hear a friend's voice. I'm sorry I caused so much trouble. I'm sorry there's been all this publicity about the gym. I hope we can still be friends. You're the only one I feel close to anymore."

In Amy's second month in jail, two new young women entered the junior tier. Having company helped a little. Amy began to realize her release was probably not imminent. "I just hope," she wrote to Paul, "I can be home for my birthday." If not, Amy wondered if prison guards would allow her to have a cake. She included a picture she had colored of Mickey Mouse, with a smiling face in the corner. "See you soon, pal," she wrote across the drawing.

Meanwhile Elliot and Rose Fisher struggled to remain strong. They spoke with Naiburg several times a day, resolved to continue the fight to arrange their daughter's bail. The trial seemed distant: right now, Amy's parents simply wanted their daughter home.

The couple's families rallied around them. After hearing the news about Amy, several relatives the Fishers had not spoken to in years called to offer support. Amy told Paul it was the only good thing to come out of her arrest: at last her parents had been reunited with the rest of the family.

The Fishers leaned on Christine Edwards-Neumann. The attorney had begun dropping by the house almost every night after Amy's arrest. On one of the worst nights of all—when "A Current Affair" broadcast its Lolita tapes—Edwards-Neumann was on hand to help them through. Seeing his daughter giggling in bed with a paying customer was more than Elliot Fisher could bear. It was one of the few times Amy's father broke down and sobbed.

Edwards-Neumann was also there to comfort Rose when a *Newsday* story erroneously referred to Amy's arrest for murder. Rose Fisher wept when she read it. The mistake cut deep.

"It's Freudian," the attorney told her with a hug. "The DA's office is treating this like a murder case."

Repeatedly the attorney reassured the Fishers that Amy's high bail did not mean the teenager wouldn't get a fair trial. "Remember," she'd say, "in the final analysis, although you have a gentleman in black robes up there with a gavel, this is going to be turned over to twelve people who have children, life experiences, and questions they want answers to."

The struggle to make Amy's bail continued. In mid-July Rose Fisher and Eric Naiburg drove to Newark, New Jersey, for a meeting with a wealthy bondsman, Philip Konvitz. The eighty-year-old grandfather, chairman of the International Fidelity Insurance Co., had been following Amy's case in the newspapers.

Rose Fisher told Konvitz that she and her husband would put up everything they had to get Amy out of jail—almost $1 million. She begged him to put up the rest.

"You're giving up all your life savings," he said. "Do you realize that?"

"I know it," said Rose, "but my daughter is not going anywhere."

Normally the fee for a $2 million bond would be 10 percent—or $200,000.

A businessman all his life, Philip Konvitz did what he always had done: he went by instinct. He saw the pain in Rose Fisher's eyes, the love she had for her daughter—no matter what kind of trouble the child had created. He knew Rose was a caring, compassionate parent. Konvitz thought about his own daughter. Rose Fisher was just about her age. The elderly man stood and motioned to Eric Naiburg.

"You," he said, pointing. "Come with me."

The attorney followed him out into the hallway. "You want to talk out here?" Naiburg asked, puzzled.

"I sold bonds on the street corner in 1941—I like to stand on a corner doing business," he quipped. "Now look me in the eye. Is this kid going to run?"

Eric Naiburg was adamant. "She's not going anywhere."

When they walked back into the conference room, Philip Konvitz looked at Rose and nodded. "We'll go with it."

Rose Fisher smiled, and her eyes filled with tears. She kissed him on the cheek.

"Thank you," she said quietly.

Konvitz opened a bottle of wine; the group toasted the deal.

Later, when the press called Konvitz for a comment, the elderly man was terse.

"I don't know if Amy is guilty or not," he said. "I don't care. I did it for the parents."

It took days to hammer out the appropriate papers. When it was all ready, Konvitz pocketed $100,000 and wrote a bail bond for $2 million. As collateral the Fishers put up their house, assessed at $400,000, stocks and bonds valued at $475,000, and $300 in cash.

When the papers were ready, Eric Naiburg presented it to Fred Klein and Judge Goodman. Throughout the day various parties in the bond arrangement arrived, consulted, and signed numerous papers. At one point in the judge's chambers, Fred Klein asked Chris Edwards-Neumann about Konvitz's $100,000 fee. Did it come from the Fishers' bank account? She said it did.

True, but misleading. Of the $100,000, $40,000 was indeed from the Fishers. It was the remaining $60,000 that may have killed the deal. The money was put up by KLM Productions of Smithtown, a little-known investment group on Long Island. KLM had bought exclusive rights to Amy's story for a movie deal. As part of their contract the company also had exclusive rights to all publishing and broadcast interviews. The company also agreed to pay the Fishers an additional $20,000 if they made a movie, to offset the $40,000 Amy's parents had paid toward the bond.

Eric Naiburg's Hollywood knight had actually come through.

But Fred Klein and Judge Goodman didn't know about the movie connection. In his chambers, around 3:00 P.M., Judge Goodman signed the bail bond.

When Naiburg at last had the receipt, he walked over to Rose Fisher and kissed her hand. Outside the courtroom, he held out the receipt for reporters. "It's home free now," he said. "You see this? It's get out of jail. Unfortunately it's not free."

As the Fishers and Naiburg headed to the Nassau County Correctional Facility to pick up Amy, reporters rushed to trail them. Fox News managed to get an emotional response from Amy's mother.

"To people who think you shouldn't put up everything for this, what do you tell them?" reporter Eric Shawn asked.

"That they can't know what it's like to be a parent," Rose Fisher snapped, then broke into tears.

When Amy emerged from jail, few recognized her. A day earlier another young inmate had braided the teenager's long, thick hair in cornrows. Wearing the same blue cutoffs and white T-shirt she'd had on sixty-one days before, when she was picked up by homicide detectives, Amy cupped her hands over her face in Naiburg's white Mercedes. It sped out of the jail at 4:40 P.M.

That evening, camera crews waited impatiently for the family's arrival at home in Merrick. Rose and Elliot Fisher arrived home first, driving directly into the garage. A few minutes later, Rose Fisher taped newspaper over the garage windows. When Amy and Naiburg arrived, they, too, drove into the garage, and disappeared from sight.

Inside the house, Amy immediately picked up Muffin, hugging her tight. The little dog barked wildly. Amy went up to her room. It looked the same. She took a shower. When she walked downstairs, wearing jeans and a white T-shirt with a giant red strawberry, Eric Naiburg looked up and laughed. "I don't even recognize you," he said.

Around 9 P.M., the Fishers stepped outside and the cameras began to flash. Standing in the driveway, a beaming Amy Fisher hugged her mother and waved to reporters. The Fishers, Naiburg, his wife, June, and Edwards-Neumann and her husband drove to Villa Rosa, an Italian restaurant in Freeport, just down the block from Stitch n' Sew. Amy feasted on veal parmigiana and spaghetti.

At home that night, Amy brushed past reporters and hurried inside. Her future was unsettled, her punishment unknown; but tonight Amy Fisher would sleep soundly in her own room next to her mom and dad. For all the times she'd tearfully threatened to run away, that night Amy Fisher basked in the joy of coming home.

Chapter
Twenty-Four

For two months Mary Jo had been comforted by knowing Amy remained behind bars. But when the teenager walked out of the Nassau County Correctional Facility, the Massapequa housewife took the news badly.

It had been a busy week. The family's attorneys, after weeks of negotiations, had finally brought Mary Jo a contract to sign, selling the movie rights to her story. Of the sixteen production companies vying for the deal, she had selected Tri-Star Television. After myriad meetings with the company's representatives, Mary Jo believed Tri-Star would portray a sympathetic account of the story, based on what had happened to her. What the housewife didn't want was a scathing saga of Joey's adulterous relationship with her adolescent assailant.

Although the lawyers announced a deal worth several hundred thousand dollars and said it could eventually pay more than $1 million if a miniseries resulted and home video sales and other rights were included, Tri-Star reportedly will pay Mary Jo Buttafuoco just under $300,000 if it makes the film. Joey, too, sold his rights to the movie company, but for a nominal fee. The movie, all insist, is Mary Jo's story, and the money is needed to pay for her prodigious medical bills, now topping $100,000.

The day after announcing the deal, Rindenow and Kornberg labored over the contract in Rindenow's East Meadow office. Shortly before 2:00 P.M. they received a jarring phone call.

"There's a meeting in ten minutes in Judge Goodman's chambers," a source said. "I think bail has been posted for Amy."

Rindenow immediately dialed the Nassau County pressroom. One of the reporters, an old friend, picked up the phone.

"So what's going on there today?" Rindenow asked nonchalantly.

"Pretty quiet day," the reporter answered.

"Hmm," said Rindenow. "Why don't you go check Judge Goodman's chambers? Amy may be getting out."

"Holy shit!" came the reply. "I'll get right back to you."

The next call Rindenow made was to the Buttafuoco home. He prayed Mary Jo wouldn't hear of Amy's release from a reporter.

Michael Rindenow drummed his fingertips on the desk impatiently as the phone rang repeatedly. Frustrated, he tried Complete Auto Body. Caspar Buttafuoco told him Mary Jo, Joey, and the kids were relaxing at the beach club.

When the attorney finally reached the couple,

Joey took the news about Amy's release calmly. Mary Jo, however, began to weep hysterically.

"I can't believe it," she said. "What about me? What about my safety? What about my children? What about my husband?"

Rindenow tried to console her. He assured her that the police would provide protection.

"Mary Jo," he added, "I think it's in our best interest to call a press conference. You need to be able to say your side of all this."

Tearful, Mary Jo agreed. Rindenow and Kornberg spread the word: Mary Jo Buttafuoco would respond at a news conference at 6:00 P.M.

Reporters who had staked out the Nassau County Correctional Facility to catch a glimpse of Amy and Naiburg speeding out of the prison gate hurried to Rindenow's office for the next installment of the story. Before Mary Jo arrived, Rindenow sternly issued ground rules. He warned the crowd to keep questions geared toward Mary Jo's feelings about the release or her medical condition. No queries about Joey or the affair would be permitted.

More than fifty journalists and photographers jammed the parking lot. Less than a mile away, Mary Jo and Joey sat in a traffic tie-up caused by dozens of camera crew vans. As they waited at a red light, Mary Jo nudged Joey.

"Give me a pen," she said.

On a scrap of paper the housewife scribbled a short statement. Minutes later, by the side door of the law office, she read it aloud.

"What has happened to me physically, mentally, and emotionally can never be changed," Mary Jo said. "My hope is now while Amy Fisher is out on bail she and her parents make good use of her time, and consider obtaining for her some serious psychological help. In my opinion, she needs it."

For the next few minutes Mary Jo took questions. She showed reporters the four-inch scar along her neck and discussed her ailments—the deafness, double vision, and partial paralysis. Prompted by a reporter's question, Mary Jo spoke of her fears.

"I won't feel safe again until she's behind bars," she said. "I just know what this girl did to me, in cold blood. Anybody who'd do that is a sick person. She's a sick girl."

Mary Jo dismissed rumors of an impending breakup. Her marriage, she maintained, was unimpaired. "We're a strong family," she said. "We were strong before this happened. We're a tight family—this won't change us, Joe, myself, and the kids."

When told Amy Fisher was celebrating her release on bail with an Italian dinner, Mary Jo pointed to her throat caustically. "Oh, is that right?" she said. "I can't have a fine Italian meal. My esophagus is paralyzed; I'm living on baby food. So tell her to have a bite for me."

Later, at home, Mary Jo stepped out on her front lawn and chatted with reporters. She put her arm around Jessica. "I want everyone here to know that this is *my* daughter," she said, "and I'm proud of *my* daughter."

The next day Amy Fisher was back in court. Judge Goodman planned to issue an order of protection forbidding her from having any contact with Mary Jo Buttafuoco or any member of the Buttafuoco family. What was expected to be a routine hearing, however, turned raucous.

Minutes after the bailiff called the court in session, Fred Klein lashed out, complaining that Chris Edwards-Neumann had misled him. The assistant district attorney said he had specifically asked who had put up the bail bondsman's $100,000 fee. That very morning he had learned the truth about the money—that a movie company had contributed $60,000 in return for Amy's story.

The mood in the courtroom turned tense. Edwards-Neumann, in the first row, grasped Rose Fisher's hand. Amy's mother began to cry softly. In front of the judge, Amy, too, was beginning to panic. She wasn't sure what all of this meant. Fred Klein was railing, and Naiburg suddenly seemed nervous. The teenager listened with growing alarm.

"It is very odd to me that all this financial information was jammed down our throats yesterday afternoon at two o'clock but no mention at all was made about a production company being involved," Klein thundered. "In no place in any of the paperwork does it say that any of the money came from a production company or movie rights. . . . I asked that woman yesterday where the hundred thousand dollars came from. She knew that part of the premium of sixty thousand dollars was put up by a production company, but she never told me that and she never told the court that."

Judge Goodman glared at Naiburg. "The court should be informed of everything," he growled.

Fred Klein wasn't finished. "I think that is against the public policy of this state to allow defendants to sell their rights to how they committed a crime and then profit by that by getting a bail bond," he said. "I think that it is improper."

Amy pulled on Naiburg's jacket. The attorney leaned over. "Are they going to send me back?" she whispered.

Naiburg didn't answer. He put his arm around Amy and cradled her head on his lap. It was an affecting scene. As Amy blinked back tears, her attorney fought for her freedom.

"She is presumed innocent, Your Honor," he practically shouted. "That is the foundation, the premise, the basis, of our entire judicial system. Let me have my client back so I can prepare her defense. There's nothing against public policy, there's nothing wrong with it. She is here, Judge. Please don't deprive her of her liberty."

It was a close call for Amy. In a silent courtroom, Judge Goodman gave his ruling: the bail money was acceptable.

He then issued a stern warning. "Amy Fisher."

"Yes?"

"As a condition of your release on bail you are directed to stay away from the home of and to refrain from any contact with Mary Jo Buttafuoco and all members of her family. I wish to make it very clear that if you, Amy Fisher, do not obey this order of protection, a contempt proceeding will be held, and after the hearing if it is found that you have willfully failed to obey this order, I shall revoke your bail and commit you back to the custody of the sheriff of the county of Nassau. Do you understand that?"

"Yes, Your Honor."

It was over. Amy Fisher's next court date: September 14, for a pretrial hearing. It would be the day before her father's fifty-seventh birthday.

Climbing into the family's station wagon that morning, Amy was visibly shaken. Scores of journalists surrounded the car. The pressure was too much. Amy bent her head to her lap and sobbed.

Fifteen minutes later she and her mother pulled up in front of their home. Elliot Fisher opened the door for his family. Without glancing at the media camped on the sidewalk, he closed the door and double-locked it.

For the rest of the day reporters lingered outside the Fisher home. Now and then one would tap lightly on the front door, only to be turned away. The family, Rose Fisher said firmly, was not talking to anyone.

The door did open once that afternoon. A young police officer from the nearby seventh precinct, on duty since 7:15 A.M., needed to use the bathroom— badly. Around noon he knocked gingerly.

On the front stoop, he spoke to Rose Fisher for several minutes. Reporters watching from the sidewalk began to joke that even a cop who had to go to the bathroom couldn't enter the fortress.

He did. Rose had only been complaining about the press on the sidewalk.

"When is all this going to stop?" she asked, gesturing to the camera crews. "I don't know what they're waiting for. We're not going anywhere."

Rose Fisher has been true to her word. Since Amy has been released on bail, the family seldom ventures out of their home. In the evenings Elliot Fisher drives to the video store and picks up an armful of tapes for his daughter. Rose spends hours preparing Amy's favorite meals. Dining on stuffed pasta shells and bread, Amy is slowly regaining the weight she lost in jail.

Sometimes, after dusk, the Fishers take their daughter out for a drive. Once they met relatives and walked along the boardwalk in Long Beach. In the darkness passersby didn't recognize the Merrick teenager.

Amy sees a counselor regularly and meets sporadically with Naiburg in his Hauppage office. But Amy is never alone. For many months this crafty young girl managed to lead a clandestine life that almost destroyed her family and the Buttafuocos. Her mistakes and misshaped judgment caused many—especially an innocent woman—irreparable harm.

Now, one of her parents is always by her side. With their daughter's freedom and everything they own at stake, Elliot and Rose Fisher are taking no chances.

Chapter Twenty-Five

In the two months Amy spent in jail, many changes occurred at home. Her parents' lifelong business was gone. A few days after the arrest, Rose Fisher had penciled a note and taped it to the front door of Stitch 'n Sew: "Sorry for any inconvenience. Will reopen soon."

It never did. In early June Elliot and Rose told their landlord they might close the shop. Two weeks later they made it official. Meeting in the landlord's office in his marine supply store two doors away, Elliot and Rose explained that they needed to devote all their energy to getting Amy out on bail. Then there'd be the trial to endure. Stitch 'n Sew would have to go.

Their landlord felt bad. He liked the couple. Over the years he'd enjoyed little chats with Elliot in front of their respective stores when stepping outside for fresh air. Rose always gave him a friendly smile and wave when he passed by.

For nineteen years the Fishers had been dependable tenants, paying rent promptly the first of the month. Stitch 'n Sew was a bit cluttered—choked with enormous pieces of foam rubber poised to topple to the floor—but that hadn't been a problem. The landlord knew he'd lose several months' rent until he found new renters, but he didn't say anything. He felt sorry for the Fishers. He wished them well.

Over the next two weeks Amy's parents cleared the shop, trying to sell and store as much inventory as they could. To some regular customers, Rose mentioned that she would do custom work from home. The Fishers said a warm good-bye to their mailman. Such a nice family, he thought as he shook Elliot Fisher's hand.

Even though the couple ran Stitch 'n Sew on the corner of Church Street and Merrick Road in downtown Freeport for almost two decades, they didn't know many other merchants on the block. That didn't stop the others from trading the latest news on the Fisher family. "What a shame," they all said. "Such hardworking people."

Nineteen years of labor, gone. Chris Edwards-Neumann typed up a letter of dissolution for the business. Reading the document, Elliot Fisher swallowed painfully. He wondered how much more the family could endure.

Amy Fisher returned home one month after her classmates graduated from John F. Kennedy High School. She had one term paper to submit, and she, too, would receive a diploma.

She'd missed a lot: not only the graduation

242

ceremony, but all the preceding senior class festivities, including a beach outing, a pizza party, and the prom. She didn't get an opportunity to buy the yearbook, "Signs of the Times." While seniors passed their yearbooks among friends, writing memories of the last four years and their dreams for the future, Amy Fisher was holed up in a tiny cell at the Nassau County Correctional Facility, charged with attempted murder. Perhaps fittingly, under Amy's yearbook picture there was no caption.

Amy's arrest had caused tremendous disorder in the school. Within days the media invaded the parking lot and the sidewalk in front of the school. Rumors began circulating that because of the overbearing press attention, the graduation ceremony would be moved indoors—to the gym. Bitterness was widespread.

"It isn't fair," said one seventeen-year-old girl. "What she did has nothing to do with graduation. It will ruin it. Inside we only get a few tickets. Outside, it's unlimited. Everybody's upset."

Teachers at the high school pressed students to remember their responsibilities. Regents exams were just a few weeks away. "They're always saying 'Come on guys, we have to learn,'" said one senior. "They keep saying 'Forget the cameras. Your work is what's important.'"

Throughout the halls of John F. Kennedy, "Amy" jokes spread swiftly. "The favorite joke is, 'If you don't take gym, you can't graduate, but if you shoot someone, that's okay,'" recounted one senior. "Or else these retards go around singing, 'Amy's Gotta Gun,' like that song."

It was hard to concentrate. Television crews lined the sidewalk every afternoon, eager to film anyone who'd talk about Amy. A chance to appear on the evening news was tempting. Sophomores who'd never heard of Amy Fisher before her arrest trooped up to the cameras and spoke out. "What kind of thirty-six-year-old man goes out with a seventeen-year-old girl?" one crowed. "Obviously there's something wrong with him. He's old enough to be her father."

One young man almost made a career out of Amy. Seth Frankel, eighteen, who lived down the block from the Fishers, rapidly managed to anoint himself the resident expert. He appeared on "Geraldo," "9 Broadcast Plaza," and "Hard Copy" and was interviewed for a radio show. He usually demanded payment for his information but just as quickly dropped the requirement if money wasn't forthcoming. Eager to get on television and in the newspapers, Frankel usually gave a standard reply to questions about Amy: "She was a weird girl."

A nervous, high-strung young man, Frankel stretched his fragments of information about Amy to ridiculous lengths, and when he wasn't sure about something, he guessed. Amy's bedroom, he reported, was pink, with flowers. It isn't. It's light gray. He told Geraldo he'd seen pornographic pictures of Amy and her boyfriends. Nope. Not true.

In the driveway of his waterfront home one

afternoon, a few weeks after Amy's arrest, Frankel pointed with pride to the sagging basketball net hanging in the driveway. "See that?" he said. "Geraldo broke it. He was here. Really. I played ball with him."

Frankel boasted that his picture in the yearbook, under Frankel, is right next to Amy's, Fisher, as if that proved he knew her better than anyone else. No one in the neighborhood or at John F. Kennedy High School ever saw Amy Fisher even speak to Seth Frankel. Indeed, Merrick youths laugh when the young man's name is mentioned in connection with Amy. Frankel's parents, though, don't find it funny.

After a few weeks of cameras trained on the Frankel home, neighbors began complaining to Seth's parents. Humiliated, the couple began shooing away reporters. "We don't even know the girl," Seth's mother shouted. "Now my neighbors are giving me the business. Leave us alone."

Turning to her son, she snapped, "Get in the house."

One less rider on the Amy Fisher bandwagon.

Despite the Frankel episode, support for Amy was strong among those who really did know her. At her high school, groups of classmates talked about a fun-loving girl brainwashed by an older man. It was Joey Buttafuoco, they believed, who was ultimately responsible for what had happened. On Merrick Road, about a mile from the high school, local kids spray-painted "Pro-Amy" on an office building. Below, they scribbled, "Where's Butta?"

At Future Physique the sentiment was the same. Those who remembered Amy from workouts described a dainty girl in stretch bodysuits who had fallen under the spell of a much older man.

"She looked like a little kid," recalled one man who trained there. "No makeup, very plain. Quiet. No one's condoning what she did—that's wrong. But everybody thinks there were greater forces at work than she could handle."

That's what Maria Murabito thinks, too. The young girl, one of Amy's closest friends, fought hard for Amy's reputation in the first weeks following the arrest. Maria and two of Amy's other friends had gone to the jail immediately after hearing of the arrest. (The prison is just a few minutes' drive from Maria's North Bellmore home, where she lives with her parents.) In her Camaro, with an "Italian Princess" sign in the front window, Maria turned off Hempstead Turnpike onto Carman Avenue in East Meadow. She eyed the gray buildings surrounded by barbed wire. It was an eerie place, no doubt.

The teenagers pulled up the north gate and drove past a large gold-and-white sign. "You are now entering the Nassau County Correctional Facilities." Below, the same words were written in Spanish.

"We're here to see Amy Fisher," Maria explained.

"Amy Fisher is only seeing family," the guard said.

Disappointed, the threesome walked back to the car, pondering what to do next. Across the street they saw the back building of the Nassau County Medical Center. They knew Joey Buttafuoco would be there, playing the devoted husband.

Maria was sick inside. She'd met Joey several times when she was with Amy and had heard enough about him to last the rest of her life. She believed he had twisted her friend's mind, and now Amy was in a terrible mess.

She decided to confront him. Later she'd insist she was simply visiting a cousin who happened to be on the same floor as Mary Jo Buttafuoco. Whatever her true motives, on the eighth floor of the hospital, outside Mary Jo's room, Maria and her two friends bumped squarely into Joey Buttafuoco.

He glowered when he saw her. His family and the Connerys were milling around, in and out of Mary Jo's room. Joey was not happy to see his lover's pals. They knew too much, way too much. Joey knew the drill: the best defense is a good offense.

"What are you doing here?" he thundered. "I'm calling security."

Maria, a tiny girl of just four feet ten inches, didn't flinch before the burly repairman. She walked right up to him, barely reaching his chest. She met his icy stare with disdain. "You're going to get yours," she hissed, then turned and headed to the elevator.

Joey asked a hospital employee to call security. He demanded a guard follow the teenagers into the elevator and out of the hospital. That same day the Buttafuocos requested that Mary Jo be transferred to a more secure location. She was— to a room next to the nurses' station at the end of the hall.

Despite Maria's allegiance to her friend, the episode on the eighth floor of the Nassau County Medical Center would prove detrimental to Amy's defense. In his bail argument Assistant District Attorney Fred Klein used the hospital incident as an example that the Buttafuocos would be in profound danger if Amy were released.

"A threat was made against a member of the Buttafuoco family only a few days after the defendant was arrested," he said. "A friend of hers, a very good friend of the defendant, visited her in the Nassau County jail. She then went over to the hospital, right from the jail, to Mrs. Buttafuoco's hospital room, and she confronted a member of the family outside of the hospital room and made a threat against that member of the family."

Maria was distraught. It hadn't been that way at all. A day later, when a reporter knocked on the door of her parents' home, Maria tried to explain. "He was the one who threatened me," she said of Joey.

Maria began to tell of the flower deliveries from Joey and how he often professed his love for Amy. But suddenly her mother appeared at the door and practically dragged the young girl away.

That night the Murabitos warned their daughter that she was not helping Amy by talking about the case. Later Maria spoke by telephone with Elliot and Rose Fisher. The threesome agreed that when the time was right they would speak out on behalf of Amy. For now it was best to stay quiet—even amid the scurrilous headlines that hurt so deeply.

When approached by a reporter a few weeks later, Maria retreated. She looked sad, glancing behind her nervously, worried her parents would hear. She smiled ruefully.

"It was worth a try," she said to the disappointed journalist. "I just can't. Those who really know her won't talk."

Chapter
Twenty-Six

Almost as soon as Mary Jo Buttafuoco regained consciousness she began to worry about her children. As time passed she noticed that Paul and Jessica seemed to handle the upheaval in their lives with amazing resilience. Yet she suspected the children harbored deeper, more troubling feelings that had not yet surfaced.

While Mary Jo recovered in the hospital, nine-year-old Jessica crayoned a poignant card:

Dear Mom,
   I miss you a whole lot. The detectives know where the person who did that to you lives. You'll be out of the hospital in a jiffy. I love you very much and I will give up my life for you.
Love, Jessica.

After the shooting, Paul and Jessica stayed home from school for almost three weeks. They watched news vans pull up to the house every morning and took phone messages from assorted journalists. Once, when a reporter called after Amy Fisher's arrest, Paul explained that his father would not comment. He sounded much older than twelve. Before hanging up, the sixth-grader added, "My mom's going to be okay. That's all I care about." A few days later the boy emerged from the house wearing dark sunglasses and holding a video camera. As photographers rushed to snap his picture, Paul raised the camera and began filming the photographers.

When Mary Jo returned from the hospital, she told Paul and Jessica they could help her by behaving, doing their schoolwork, and praying for Mommy. Every evening the children curled up in bed next to her, talking about their day.

Joey began driving them back to school in early June and reminded both children that they were responsible for their homework. "There are no free rides," he said firmly. "I expect you to study hard."

Joey and Mary Jo tried to give the children opportunities to talk about their feelings. On a few occasions Joey attempted to explain what had happened. "Amy Fisher shot your mother," he said. "She is a sick person. There are good people and there are bad people."

Later he added to reporters, "They watch television, they know what I'm talking about."

One night Joey took his kids to an open house at their school. Teachers told him the children were holding up well. Joey felt proud. His kids were tough, Buttafuocos through and through. When Paul graduated from sixth grade a few days later, the Buttafuoco family applauded loudly from the audience. That day they held a family celebration. Although it was draining for Mary Jo, she was there to hug her son and tell him how proud she was of him. As much as she could, Mary Jo Buttafuoco wanted to ensure her children's lives remained as normal as possible.

The kindness and support of the Biltmore Shores community made an enormous difference for Mary Jo Buttafuoco. A friend, Maria, began organizing a rotating schedule of neighbors to prepare home-cooked meals—meats and pasta, fish and salads. The neighbors also banded together to watch Paul and Jessica when Joey was at the hospital.

The Lakewood Florist Shop on Merrick Road stayed busy, delivering more than a dozen flower arrangements to One Adam Road West. As the flowers began to wilt, Joey brought them outside, lining the pots along the grass, notes from well-wishers still attached.

St. Rose of Lima, the Buttafuocos' parish, offered special prayers for Mary Jo during mass. The church also included her name on the list of the sick read out loud by parish priests.

Even owners of the beach club next door helped out. They fashioned a makeshift entrance through a fence at the side of the Buttafuoco home, which made getting to the club easier for

Mary Jo. The new entrance also helped her avoid photographers stationed in front of her house.

Neighbors, too, began to shoo away reporters. As weeks passed, and journalists continued to canvas the neighborhood, writing articles about Joey's past drug use and new charges in the Amy affair, Biltmore Shore residents began to retreat. One afternoon, planting flowers in pots on the front lawn, Josephine Slattery, in glasses and a kerchief, approached angrily. Clearly she had had enough.

"I just want peace and quiet," she snapped. "There's too many reporters around here and it's not necessary. It's needless. They're wonderful people. I just want to see their family back to the way it was."

At the beach club, residents were equally evasive. A few, however, concede they aren't sure what to make of Joey.

"It's their business," said a man who lives down the street from the Buttafuocos. "It's between the two of them, whatever happened. We're tired of all this. It's not why we moved here, any of us. It's not our business. They've got to deal with it."

"We stick together," a young woman added, jostling her baby on her lap. "We're a very close neighborhood. If they want to talk about it, fine. If they don't, that's okay too."

Mary Jo Buttafuoco did talk about what happened to her and how she felt—only the conversation did not stay within the confines of Biltmore Shores. One afternoon, about a week after Mary Jo returned home from the hospital, five neighborhood women gathered in her home, sipping coffee and listening sympathetically. One was listening especially closely. The woman, identified later as Bonnie Miller, wore a concealed tape recorder. She was about to make a lot of money.

Mary Jo talked. She talked about Amy Fisher, about how Joey never realized the young girl was obsessed with him. She talked about her fears and her pain. She railed about Eric Naiburg's attempts to sell Amy's story for bail money.

Bonnie Miller reportedly sold the tape to "Hard Copy" for $16,000. A few days later Mary Jo's private musings played to millions of entranced listeners.

"Apparently she was obsessed with him, apparently, but never told him. In her own mind, in her own sick, warped mind. She never came on to him. That is what is so bizarre. It was totally fantasized in her head. So I said to Joe, 'Are you sure that maybe she did and you just never realized it? Are you that thick in the skull? We all have a little kidding around, flirting, putting your arm around.' . . . Never cheat. He said, 'She never touched me. She never looked at our pictures and said, 'Oh, you can do better than that,' or 'Oh, Joey wouldn't it be nice if . . . Nothing.'

"It was totally fantasized in her head, and she's telling this to her lawyer. She's telling this to her lawyer, so that's where these stories come from. From her sick head. This was a girl's fantasy mind, that's all it is. Everything that she is saying is in a fantasy. And obviously she really fantasized it, because coming here to try to kill me, thinking that she could get Joey . . . She was obsessed with him in her own sick, warped mind. . . . I think I talked to you about my fear about going home when I was in the hospital. I'm afraid to go out my front stoop. . . . I get down every once in a while when I look in the mirror, or I see a picture of myself in the paper with my face all droopy, and I feel a little sorry for myself, but I'm on heavy narcotics so I cry easily, you know, but that's because it's just the pills. . . . I'm talking. Don't mind me, you know. (*She cries*) What is this country coming to? This woman tries to kill me and she is going to sell her story? They're going to sell her story to get her out of jail? Isn't there a law against profiting?"

Mary Jo wept as she heard her words on television. She felt she would never again know whom to trust. Miller also allegedly supplied a video of Mary Jo and Joey dancing at a Labor Day party at the Biltmore Shores Beach Club the year before, at the peak of his affair with Amy Fisher. Joey, wearing an unbuttoned shirt, rocked cozily with his wife and joined a buoyant conga line in the recreation room of the club.

At an impromptu press conference at the courthouse a few weeks later, Marvyn Kornberg announced he had filed a privacy violation complaint with the Federal Communications Commission against WCBS (Channel 2) and "Hard Copy." "Mary Jo has been victimized on two occasions," he said. "Once by Amy Fisher when she was shot in the head and once by a friend who stabbed her in the back." Kornberg boasted it was he who figured out who had surreptitiously taped the conversation. When pressed for details, he just grinned. "If I told you, you'd know as much as me."

It was the first of many legal maneuvers filed by the Buttafuoco lawyers. Days after Amy was released on bail, Rindenow filed a $125 million lawsuit against Amy, her parents, and Peter Guagenti. The lawsuit seeks $25 million in compensatory damages and $50 million in punitive damages against Amy; $25 million against her parents and $25 million against Peter Guagenti, for driving Amy to the Buttafuoco home and selling her the gun.

Rindenow also attempted to seize the $60,000 the Fishers received from KLM Productions and used to pay the bail bondsman's fee. He told reporters he was not looking to revoke Amy's bail, but rather to attach the money and profits Amy might make from a movie or book for Mary Jo's medical bills.

At a show-cause hearing, the Buttafuoco lawyers began telling the court how Mary Jo's life had been shattered by Amy. Supreme Court Justice Edward Hart quelled their attempt quickly. "She is presumed innocent," he said of Amy, interrupting the lawyer. "Counselor, save your breath. It's absolutely irrelevant."

Hart, however, issued a temporary restraining order prohibiting the transfer of any more money

257

to the Fishers from KLM or any other movie company or book publisher.

All the legal wrangling was exhausting for Mary Jo. She wondered how she would make it through the trial. Again she asked wearily, "When is this all going to end?"

Chapter
Twenty-Seven

Joey's schmoozing with the press on the front lawn of One Adam Road West stopped immediately after the Howard Stern debacle. Kornberg, shrewd and media savvy, worked hard to tidy the repairman's image.

It wasn't easy. Since the shooting, Joey had been hard to muzzle. When he spoke to the media even his closest friends cringed.

"She's absolutely fucking nuts," he usually said when asked about Amy. "I didn't know she was a whore. I didn't know she was nuts. My wife said, 'Couldn't you tell she was nuts?' The truth is, I never thought she was nuts."

Perhaps the most intriguing response from Joey came after a reporter asked what exactly he had told detectives about his relationship with the high school senior. Joey Buttafuoco explained eagerly.

"I said to them, 'If a guy screws a sixteen-year-old, what happens?'" he said. "The detective said,

'Nothing, absolutely nothing.' So I said, 'If a guy screws a seventeen-year-old girl, what happens?' And the detective said, 'Nothing, absolutely nothing.' And that's when I said, 'Okay, I know her.' And that's all I told them on that count. And if they have a tape or recording with me saying I screwed her, let them produce it."

Once Marvyn Kornberg took over, the press began to see less of Joey. The repairman was noticeably absent when Mary Jo spoke out about Amy's release on bail. When Kornberg and Rindenow announced the Buttafuocos had negotiated a movie deal, it was Mary Jo who signed the lucrative contract.

Not that the repairman gave up center stage without a fight. Once, shortly after Kornberg was hired, the attorney interrupted an interview to take a call from Joey. Clearly Marvyn Kornberg has had more cooperative clients.

"No, no, no," the attorney practically shouted into the phone. "Don't talk to anyone. No. Joey, listen. Don't worry about the momentum. Listen to me. No, no, no."

Joey did get another opportunity to sit down with the press. Kornberg arranged for the repairman and his wife to give an exclusive interview with the *Post*'s McAlary.

"I owed him a favor," Kornberg explained to a crowd of reporters.

It must have been a big one. The story presented, for the first time, Mary Jo's brutal account of the morning of May 19 as well as Joey's reaction to hostility he has faced from an unsympathetic public. In the interview, Joey sounded woeful.

"This could happen to anybody—I mean, you just never know," he said. "I never knew the kid was nuts. She shoots my wife and now I'm getting killed. I feel like Rocky after eight rounds. I'm getting pummeled. People hate me. My wife doesn't believe I had an affair with this girl. But even if I did—even if I was somebody else—that's no reason to shoot a guy's wife in the head."

Shortly after the *Post* annihilated its competition with McAlary's "Mary Jo's Story: The Day I Got Shot" piece, it was the broadcast media's turn. Kornberg gave the story to T Chua Chang from "Eyewitness News" on Channel 7.

Chang's exchange with Joey quickly turned feisty.

CHANG: Did you ever have sex with Amy Fisher?

JOEY: No. Absolutely not.

CHANG: You're also saying you were never alone with her. You never went out with her for pizza, or even a drink, a soda?

JOEY: I never had a prearranged meeting with her.

CHANG: So you never even touched Amy Fisher.

Joey hesitated. Kornberg to the rescue.

KORNBERG: When you say touched . . . When you hand someone something . . .

CHANG: Other than handing something, a handshake . . .

KORNBERG: Other than business dealing in the car shop.

CHANG: You know what I'm talking about. I'm talking about any sexual touching.

JOEY: That's correct. I never had any of that.

Joey was visibly annoyed. He did not like this line of questioning.

Chang moved along. He asked what Joey thought about Eric Naiburg's claim that Amy was having a difficult time in jail.

JOEY: Don't tell me Amy Fisher is suffering. Mary Jo Buttafuoco is suffering. My wife, Mary Jo, is paralyzed from the center line of her face over. Right down through the esophagus. Her throat doesn't work. She can't swallow food. She doesn't have a choice.

The reporter carefully steered the queries back to Joey's relationship with Amy.

CHANG: Did she ever ask you if you had an affair with Amy?

JOEY: Yes, she did.

CHANG: And you said?

JOEY: Absolutely not.

CHANG: And she said?

JOEY: I believe you.

CHANG: End of discussion?

JOEY: End of discussion.

Marvyn Kornberg did a good job with his new client. In a short time Joey began to use the phrase Kornberg made him repeat and memorize: "You'll have to talk to my lawyer. My lawyer is Marvyn Kornberg."

But the repairman still isn't keeping as low-key as his attorney would like. Over the summer five journalists from a Tokyo television station cruised by the Buttafuoco home in a red van. Joey waved to the camera crew and the show's production coordinator, Ann Yamamoto, who explained that the station, TV Asahi, was doing a lengthy piece on the Fisher case to air on its weekly news program, "Multi Channel," in Japan.

Joey was delighted. "You want to buy my book?" he joked. "I want to sell my book to the Japanese. It's a piece of history."

Joey's piece of history is beginning to annoy some Biltmore Shores neighbors. Despite an outward appearance of solidarity, residents are divided over Joey; some say he has gone too far.

Some Massapequa residents believe it's all a power trip: Joey enjoys playing the victim. Then they remember he isn't a victim: his wife is.

While Joey tried to stay out of the press, Eric Naiburg began piecing together Amy's defense. He hired Richie Haeg, a former Suffolk County detective and now president of Action Investigations in Coram, Long Island, to track down proof of the affair. One afternoon about six weeks after the shooting, Haeg and one of his investigators entered the lobby of the Freeport Motor Inn and Boatel. They told the manager, Chris Creamer, what they wanted—every registration card with Joey Buttafuoco's name.

Creamer asked for identification. Haeg presented a business card. The manager studied the card for a moment and sighed.

"We could subpoena you," Haeg said, friendly but matter-of-fact.

"I know."

"We have one date that we're sure of—July 2. The rest are after that—over the next nine months."

"Okay," Creamer said. "I can't look for this now. We have a daily ledger sheet where we enter all the registration cards, and then we put them in a book, tie it up, and store it. Give me a couple of days. I'll call you."

When they left, Creamer discussed the situation with the other managers. He wasn't happy about getting involved in this case. He worried that regulars might be upset to hear that the motel gave out information on a client. That wouldn't be good news for those who had something to hide. But Creamer knew he didn't have a choice.

"They could definitely subpoena me, and then I'd have to do it anyway," he told the others. "Besides, it's a pain to drag your records to court. I might as well just do it now."

He looked up the July 2 date first. "Sure enough, here it is," he called out to the day manager on duty.

Creamer found five cards with the name Joe Buttafuoco. He made copies and called Haeg, who immediately sent two of his investigators to collect the evidence. Less than a week later detectives from Nassau County Homicide showed up at the motel, wanting the same information. Creamer gave them the original cards.

In his Hauppage office, Eric Naiburg held a press conference. Waving a copy of the July 2 registration card, he called on the district attorney's office to file a statutory rape charge against Joe Buttafuoco. Days later Denis Dillon's office tersely gave its response: there was not enough evidence to support the charge. The investigation, however, was still continuing.

Joey's attorney lambasted the motel receipts. Anyone, said Kornberg, could have falsely printed the repairman's name. He says his client maintains he never had an affair with Amy. That same day the *New York Post* printed results of its month-long "Who's to blame?" survey. The newspaper reported that 1,416 said Joey Buttafuoco was at fault for the shooting of Mary Jo; 324 said Amy Fisher was.

The Amy Fisher/Joey Buttafuoco imbroglio notwithstanding, Naiburg and Kornberg are not the best of friends. Shortly after Kornberg began representing Joey, the Bronx-born attorney turned down an opportunity to appear on Jackie Mason's show when he learned Naiburg, too, would be on the program.

In the lobby of the Nassau County Courthouse after Naiburg's attempts to get Amy's bail reduced had failed, Kornberg, surrounded by journalists, derided the Suffolk County attorney, listing legal errors Naiburg had made in his appeal attempts. He also ridiculed the attorney's campaign to find a Hollywood producer to post his client's bail. "What are they going to do next, run a telethon for Amy?" Kornberg asked.

As he continued to talk, Kornberg, to the amusement of the reporters, mistakenly referred several times to Amy as "Amy Jo."

"She must be one of the family," one reporter whispered, prompting smirks all around.

Suddenly Kornberg's voice dropped. His adversary loomed a few feet away. Naiburg glared at the little group.

"Shhh, Naiburg's behind me," Kornberg whispered. "Wait till he passes."

As Eric Naiburg turned his back, waiting for a painfully slow elevator, Kornberg grabbed a reporter's copy of the *New York Post*. "Let me see that," said the lawyer. "I've got another client on page three."

Chapter
Twenty-Eight

As the attorneys prepare for what promises to be a captivating trial, Peter Guagenti is trying to forget he has an upcoming date in court. Before he met Amy Fisher, the skinny, frail young man lived an unassuming life in his parents' two-story home in Bensonhurst, Brooklyn, playing stickball, football, and basketball in the schoolyard and hanging out on his front stoop with friends.

Now Peter Guagenti is charged with criminal possession of a weapon, criminal sale of a weapon, and hindering prosecution. He faces a maximum sentence of seven years, though as of this writing, he has not been indicted.

In some ways the Brooklyn-born young man is somewhat of an enigma: he was an honor student at John Dewey High School who briefly studied premed at Fordham University. His pride and joy was the sparkling maroon Thunderbird he used to drive Amy Fisher to Massapequa that fateful morning. Peter often spent hours waxing the car in front of his house.

Yet Peter had courted trouble in the past. As a teenager he was found guilty of criminal possession of stolen property. His records were sealed, however, because of his age. In Bensonhurst many of his neighborhood friends belonged to gangs. In those circles a .25-caliber Titan wasn't difficult to acquire.

In early May 1991, under the elevated train lines near his house, the young man, smitten by a promise of cash and hint of sex, made a pernicious deal: to supply seventeen-year-old Amy Fisher with an automatic pistol.

His family and neighbors couldn't have been more surprised. By all accounts Peter Guagenti appeared to be a good kid, someone who always seemed much younger and more naive than his twenty-one years.

Peter's parents, Italian immigrants, were traditional and strict with their children. Peter's father, Luigi, and mother, Carmelina, had both worked for years for Cabrini Medical Center. The Guagentis were hardworking and friendly. Luigi Guagenti often made homemade wine and passed out bottles to his neighbors. At Christmas the family always strung lavish lights to decorate the house. Peter's older brother, Anthony, is a city transit police officer; his big sister, Christine, works in law enforcement.

Peter's lawyer says that the young man was trying to put his life back on track when several significant events derailed him. Peter suffered a collapsed lung twice and in October 1991 underwent surgery. Then, just before Christmas, Luigi, who had only recently retired, had an accident with a tow truck. Days later the elder Guagenti died of a heart attack. Not long after that, Peter's longtime girlfriend, unable to deal with the Guagenti family's grief, broke up with him.

In the spring Peter took a part-time job as a clerk at R&S/Strauss, an auto parts store a few blocks from his home. He didn't have a stellar résumé—his parents had once helped him get a job at the hospital where they worked, and for a short time Peter had worked as a chauffeur for a limousine service.

But Peter did his job and got along with other employees in the shop. As the stories about Amy Fisher began headlining the local newspapers, no one at R&S imagined that the missing link in the case was busy ringing up sales at the cash register.

There was one prominent clue, however. About three weeks after the shooting, on the same day Amy Fisher's $2 million bail appeal was rejected by the Brooklyn Supreme Court, Peter Guagenti had a surprise visitor to the shop. It was someone he didn't want to see: Eric Naiburg.

When the attorney walked into the auto supply store that afternoon and asked for Peter, eyebrows were raised. Employees in the shop recognized Naiburg from the news.

Peter and Naiburg stepped aside and talked for about ten minutes.

When the attorney had left, Guagenti, trying to be casual, turned to his boss, Al Schweiger.

"Do you know who that was?" he asked.

"Yeah, that's that girl Amy Fisher's attorney," he replied. "What does he want?"

"Somehow he thinks I'm involved. The guy's crazy."

Schweiger laughed. How absurd. A few of the shop employees began to gossip lightheartedly. Wouldn't it be funny if Peter was involved? No one took it seriously.

A few days later the pressure was beginning to get to Peter Guagenti. He called in sick for almost a week. When he returned to work, his days of anonymity were over.

He punched out for lunch and walked to a nearby deli. It was shortly before 1:00 P.M. On the sidewalk, a block from the auto parts store, detectives from Nassau County Homicide Division pulled out badges and motioned him to a waiting car. Later that day police towed away his prized Thunderbird.

At least the suspense was over. Ever since the visit from Naiburg, Guagenti knew his chances of laying low much longer were slim. The young man told detectives that he didn't see Amy Fisher shoot Mary Jo Buttafuoco. He heard the gunshot, then saw Amy running to the car, carrying the pistol. When the interrogation was over, Peter was put behind bars, just a few cell blocks from Amy.

Things might have been far worse. Peter was not charged as an accomplice or conspirator in attempted murder. If he had been, those charges would have doubled his potential sentence to fifteen years.

At his arraignment Peter sat quietly, taking deep breaths and fighting back tears, his hands cuffed behind his back. He wore a white dress shirt and patterned gray pants.

The courtroom was packed. His mother, Carmelina, and sister, Christine, wearing mourning black in memory of Luigi Guagenti, locked arms, weeping. His older brother, Anthony, wore a black ribbon on his lapel. "To say we are shocked ain't the word for it," he told reporters. "Peter is a good kid—never been in any trouble before."

In court, Peter's attorney, John Esposito, appealed for a reasonable bail. He told Judge Daniel Palmieri of district court that Peter had been deeply scarred by his father's death a few months earlier. He mentioned the young man's recent surgery and how that, too, had had a detrimental effect on his life. Esposito also assured the court that Peter Guagenti's family was strong and tight-knit.

Assistant District Attorney Fred Klein stuck to the facts. "For three weeks and far-reaching media attention, this defendant sought to elude police and deny involvement," he shot back. "He provided Amy Fisher with the gun the day of the shooting, drove her up to the Buttafuoco home, sat there while she went up and shot Mrs. Buttafuoco in the head."

He pointed out that Guagenti had no ties to Nassau County and made no effort to come forward. Klein asked that bail be set at $100,000.

It was. Carmelina Guagenti immediately made provisions to put up her house as collateral. In a short time Peter Guagenti was back home, awaiting trial.

His neighborhood wasn't new to the press scrutiny that followed Peter's arrest. Just a few blocks away lived Gina Feliciano. On her eighteenth birthday in August 1989, she taunted a neighborhood crowd by telling them her black and Hispanic friends were coming to get them. Then along came Yusef Hawkins, a sixteen-year-old black man looking to buy a used car. An innocent passerby.

The group of white teenagers, wielding baseball bats, chased the young man to his death; in his urgency to escape, Yusef Hawkins ran in front of a car on the nearby parkway. His tormentors were eventually convicted of his murder.

For months Bensonhurst was besieged by protest rallies. Neighbors—Gina Feliciano included—were divided over the defendants.

Now Bensonhurst has Peter Guagenti.

But in this case reaction on the streets was uniform. This mess, locals say, is all Amy Fisher's fault.

The young woman, sneered an elderly Italian woman on the street, had lured Peter with sex. It was too much for the young man to turn down.

New York City's tabloids also treated Peter Guagenti sympathetically. AMY'S PAWN, *New York Newsday* proclaimed. Inside, the headline read, "Till This, Just a Guy in Love with His Car."

Even Nassau County police apparently felt compassion for the young man. One detective shook his head with a wry smile. "He thought he was going to get good sex, but what he got you could describe with the same word, but it wasn't sex," he said.

Chapter
Twenty-Nine

The trial of Amy Fisher is expected to begin in early 1993. As more evidence is unearthed, attorneys debate sundry possibilities. The central issue remains, What will Eric Naiburg argue?

Will he claim the shooting was the result of a terrible accident, as Amy told police? Or that the young girl was driven to violence after a year of emotional abuse by the victim's husband? Is he planning to try to convince jurors that Joey Buttafuoco enticed Amy to shoot his wife?

Eric Naiburg will probably argue all three points. Only one fact seems certain: the attorney is unlikely to offer an alibi defense. No one disputes that Amy Fisher was indeed present on the front stoop of Mary Jo Buttafuoco's home, gun in hand. What the trial must determine is, what was her intention that sunny May morning in Massapequa?

If it was attempted murder, as some believe, New York attorney Barry Slotnick has a suggestion for the defense: an insanity plea. Slotnick has won acquittals for some of the city's most famous defendants, including Bernhard Goetz, the tall, bespectacled man who a decade ago shot a group of black teenagers who'd tried to mug him on a New York City subway in the middle of the day.

"It has all the trappings," Slotnick said. "This may be someone who didn't perceive the nature and quality of her act, or whether what she was doing was right or wrong. For example, if you run away and hide, it sort of negates an insanity defense because it shows that you really knew what you were doing. But here she didn't hide, she didn't run to Mexico. She stuck around. It certainly might be a defense the jury would find palatable."

At the end of the summer, Nassau County police found the Titan used to shoot Mary Jo Buttafuoco. It had been tossed into a storm drain a few blocks from Amy's home on Berkley Lane.

Eric Naiburg hailed the finding, saying ballistic tests will prove the shooting was accidental.

That remains to be seen. At this point, Eric Naiburg is expected to present a diminished capacity defense, arguing that Amy, under the influence of Joe Buttafuoco, did not have the criminal intent to injure Mary Jo Buttafuoco.

The jury could convict Amy on a lesser charge—possibly reckless assault. That, many legal experts say, is probably what the defense is aiming for. In that case Amy might serve four or five years, rather than the twelve and a half to twenty-five for attempted murder.

"That's the best Eric can hope for," says Bruce Parnell, Stephen Sleeman's attorney.

How Eric Naiburg will present Amy Fisher to the twelve Nassau County men and woman who will decide her fate remains unclear. "There are a few possibilities," says Slotnick. "Here she was driven to a terrible life by this man, she was unable to perceive what she was doing. Maybe she could, in a certain sense, not formulate the intent—that's diminished capacity. That's all within the vein of possibility. There may be those who'll say, seventeen, sixteen, underage—he took advantage of her. If the tapes are to be believed, she goes into this second kind of life. How many faces does Eve have? He gave her one of those faces. She has lost her ability, her sensitivity. He made her into what she is—he deserves to be punished, and they should let her go. That's one side."

But Slotnick is quick to point out that the jury will also hear the testimony of Mary Jo Buttafuoco. The Massapequa housewife's harrowing experience and devastating physical and emotional injuries will make a strong impression on the jurors.

"That's the other side," says Slotnick, "the obvious: poor woman. Bullet in her head. Injured. Pain. Married to this guy."

The attorney leans back on his chair in his roomy office overlooking lower Manhattan. "Of course there's still another side," he said. " 'I just met her in passing. She came to my body shop. She fantasized. I never did any of that stuff. What is she, crazy? This woman was obsessed. What's that movie, *Fatal Attraction*? She was fatally attracted to me, which led to this event.' "

The bottom line, says Slotnick, is that the trial of Amy Fisher will hinge on one thing: the teenager's intent. "That's why I like insanity," he says. "What she did just doesn't fit within the norm. How she did it—eleven-forty-five A.M., not P.M. If it's P.M. you say, 'Okay, dark night,' whatever. The person that drove her—was she that secure in her confidence that he wasn't going to tell anybody? She hardly knew him. She's not working with what we call a full deck. That's something the jury can buy as a defense.

"You have to take away from the jury the word *purposefully*—no matter what the crime, attempted murder, assault, or attempted manslaughter, that's not significant. You've got to put in the jury's mind the idea that whatever happened was done as a result of the fact that she was a disturbed person who wasn't functioning properly and didn't know what she was doing. She didn't know whether it was right or wrong. She didn't know the nature and consequences of her act. She was insane. By the way, it may not be far from the truth. And it may be the truth. There was a guy that walked up to the president of the United States and shot him. Think about it. How much different was that case from this case? A jury found him not guilty. Even crazy people plan things out. Sometimes they do it with the help of gremlins."

In the end it will be up to a Nassau County jury. For Eric Naiburg, the next few months mean carefully plotting a strategy. In court papers filed at the end of August, Naiburg charged that Joey Buttafuoco began an affair with Amy when she was sixteen, introduced her to prostitution and knew there was a good chance Amy planned to shoot his wife. "Joey," he wrote, was "fully aware that there was a real and immediate danger that there might be an assault on his wife, that he instructed the defendant on the effective use of a firearm, and that he conscientiously established an alibi for the time when he knew the potential assault might take place."

But Naiburg faces a tough dilemma: if he calls Joseph Buttafuoco to the stand, the repairman will almost certainly take the Fifth Amendment. He is guaranteed the right to refuse to testify on the grounds that he may incriminate himself. Naiburg would surely question the repairman about his relationship with Amy before she turned sixteen. If Joey admits to the affair, he could be charged with statutory rape. On those grounds Joe Buttafuoco would probably testify only under the grant of immunity.

His lawyer isn't concerned. Marvyn Kornberg scorns Naiburg's allegations. Amy Fisher, he rails, is the only guilty party. "She's now scampering to place the blame on everybody else," he said. Besides, Kornberg doesn't believe Amy Fisher's case will go to trial at all. He says the teenager will probably plea-bargain to a lesser charge. But most legal experts disagree, especially those who know Eric Naiburg.

"It's not Naiburg's style," says an attorney who knows him well. "He's very competitive. Most lawyers say he'll try it no matter what. Unless Amy's parents say, 'Fuck you, we're taking the deal.' But the DA probably won't offer it anyway. They're the biggest hard-asses on the planet."

Indeed, some lawyers are saying that the Nassau County DA is not pressing statutory rape charges against Joe Buttafuoco simply to keep the heat on Amy's lawyer. "They don't like Naiburg—they think he's pompous," said one Suffolk County attorney. "They're out to show up Naiburg. That's getting taken out on Amy. Eric rubs a lot of people the wrong way."

Some say that the judge, too, may hold a grudge. When Judge Goodman presided over the Robert Golub trial several years ago, Naiburg anchored a legal segment for Channel 12, the local Long Island television station. On the show, the attorney was often critical of the judge's rulings.

The DA and the Nassau County Court deny any prejudice against Naiburg. The attorney's partner, Matthew Rosenblum, says the firm is not concerned about a backlash.

"Eric's a straight shooter," he said. "Sometimes you step on toes. The judge will be professional. Same thing with Fred Klein. Even if Fred hated Eric's guts, I believe he's professional enough to do what he thinks is right. Fred's the kind of guy that sticks the knife in you, but always in the front, never in the back. Eric's the same way."

As Slotnick puts it: "It's a colorful cast of characters. Marvyn's a great lawyer, Eric's a great lawyer. I'm sure Nassau County is putting on one of their shining lights on this case. They're all good lawyers. What somebody needs is a good jury."

Amy Fisher needs more than a good jury: she needs psychological help. Over the years her indiscriminate ways have led her on a winding road to disaster.

It is possible the trial may reveal some of the teenager's bleakest secrets. Certainly, Amy's experience at age twelve is an indication that something might have been terribly wrong.

Studies of adolescent prostitutes offer a startling finding—that almost all were victims of sex abuse.

"To think of her as spoiled is missing something—there is something more going on in this," says Dr. Leo Kron, director of child and adolescent psychiatry at St. Luke's/Roosevelt Hospital in New York City. "Most kids don't become prostitutes. They certainly don't consider murdering somebody. Studies say that adolescents who are out of control and sexually acting out very frequently have prior histories of being severely traumatized and often sexually abused."

Clearly the Merrick teenager isn't easy to understand. What Amy Fisher says is not always what she actually feels. "Fucking the tile man" at age twelve wasn't fun: it was rape. Attaching

279

herself to Joey Buttafuoco wasn't just a crush: it was her survival. Becoming a prostitute wasn't wild and adventurous, it was an odious cry for love and attention.

For Amy Fisher, losing Joey Buttafuoco meant all of her dreams crashed at once. The troubled teenager must have seen one way out: to strike back. Perhaps goaded on by her fascination with the Brooklyn gangs, she wanted to attack the woman Joey still loved—the woman Amy believed had everything.

What if Mary Jo Buttafuoco had broken down, sobbing, that morning on her front stoop when faced with Amy's charges of Joey's infidelity? It is quite possible there would never have been a shooting. Mary Jo's grief may have been enough to satisfy a disturbed young girl.

Not long after the shooting, Amy told Paul she regretted all that had happened. "I wish it was Joey going through this pain instead," she said. She also described how she felt about the Massapequa housewife that day on the stoop. "She was so mean to me," Amy said.

But a confident Mary Jo Buttafuoco brushed off the teenager's charge. She had composure, remembering her position in life, a life that felt comfortable and secure. Perhaps that was the final blow for Amy Fisher. "I felt she was dismissing me," the Merrick teenager had told police tearfully. With all the brutal apparitions in her soul, Amy Fisher was not about to be dismissed.

And so Mary Jo Buttafuoco suffers. She is the true victim of this story; wholly innocent and horribly maimed. Her pain will likely continue, her fears won't go away. It is the picture of Mary Jo, leaning on a cane, partly deaf, blind and paralyzed, that must be remembered. That, and the image of Amy Elizabeth Fisher, led to prison, her hair covering her face: accountable for her actions.

There is one more picture. Joey Buttafuoco. As he serves his wife a pureed dinner every night, drives her to the hospital for physical therapy, and witnesses her agony, perhaps his sentence is already being served.

Newlyweds Pam and Gregg Smart seemed like the perfect American couple. He was an up-and-coming young insurance executive, she the beautiful former cheerleader who now worked in the administration of the local school.

But on May 1, 1990, their idyllic life was shattered when Gregg was murdered in the couple's upscale Derry, New Hampshire townhouse—a single shot to his head. Three months later, the grieving widow was arrested and charged with the brutal crime.

In the dramatic trial that followed, a dark portrait of Pam Smart emerged—one of a cold manipulator who seduced a high school student with a striptease and then had a wild affair with him—until he was so involved with her that he was willing to do anything for her…even murder…

DEADLY LESSONS

BY EDGAR AWARD NOMINEE
KEN ENGLADE